A LITTLE BIT
AT A TIME

Secrets of Productive Quality

by Russell O. Wright

TEN SPEED PRESS
Berkeley, California

1☉
TEN SPEED PRESS
P.O. Box 7123
Berkeley, California 94707

Cover design by Fifth Street Design Associates
Text design by Faith and Folly
Illustrations © 1990 Ellen Sasaki

Library of Congress Cataloging-in-Publication Data

Wright, Russell O.
  A little bit at a time : secrets of productive quality / by
Russell O. Wright.
    p. cm.
    ISBN 0-89815-394-8
    1. Labor productivity. 2. Quality control.
3. Organizational effectiveness. I. Title.
HD57.W57 1990
658.3'14—dc20   89-77125
                                                                    CIP

Printed in the United States of America

1   2   3   4   5   6 — 94   93   92   91   90

ACKNOWLEDGMENTS

THE IDEAS in a book like this are formed by working with many people over many years. It's not practical to name them all, but I do want to acknowledge several groups of people who made contributions to this book (even if they did it unknowingly).

These groups include the microwave department at Philco (especially the intrepid souls who made the trip west to Sierra in 1971); the Sierra Electronics operation (an organization so "dynamic" that within two years of my arrival only one staff member had been there longer than me); the Ford Aerospace & Communications staff (nee Philco/Aeronutronic-Ford) in Dearborn and Detroit; and Division 45 in the Space & Communications group at Hughes (especially those who will recognize parts of this book from our all-day "strategy reviews").

More specifically, I want to thank the people who took the time to read drafts of this book and make helpful suggestions. In alphabetical order they are: Dave Baker, Don Chickering, Dick Jones, John King, Anne Lund, Al Owens, Paul Pedroni, and Larry Spicer. I also want to thank my editor, Sal Glynn, at Ten Speed Press for greatly improving the clarity and flow of the book.

Finally, I want to acknowledge the always-changing cast of the division/business operations departments in Division 45/4K who in many ways served as the final lab test for the ideas in this book—and some of whom looked down from the wall in my den as I did my prescribed number of pages each day, making sure I kept at it a little bit at a time all the time.

THIS BOOK IS DEDICATED TO HALINA

CONTENTS

PREFACE ix

SECTION I
WHAT TO DO AND HOW TO PLAN TO DO IT

1. Setting the Stage 3
2. What You Are Trying To Do 5
3. A Management Philosophy 14
4. Why Leading Beats Managing 22
5. A Total Quality Sampler 25
6. A Measures Primer 30
7. The End of the Beginning 39

SECTION II
GETTING AND KEEPING ONLY THE BEST PEOPLE

8. How To Get and Keep Only the Best 43
9. Meeting and Talking with Everyone
   One-to-One 48
10. Being in a Permanent Recruiting Mode 53
11. Recruiting at the Highest Possible Level
    —At All Levels 60
12. Reorganizing and Rotating Regularly 65
13. Transferring the Lowest 10% 70
14. Working with the Union 80

SECTION III
MAKING CLEAR WHAT NEEDS TO BE DONE

15. The Process of Making Things Clear 87
16. Doing the Whole Job 92
17. Individual Customers and Suppliers 95
18. Developing Job Measures 99
19. Setting Achievable Goals and Achieving Them 108
20. Be a Constructive Complainer 115
21. Practicing the Art of Communication 121
22. Managing By Walking Around (MBWA) 129
23. Training—The Universal Need 134
24. The Results You Expect 139

SECTION IV
LETTING THEM DO WHAT NEEDS TO BE DONE

25. How To Let Them Do It 147
26. Matrix Management Organizations—Theory and Reality . 149
27. Making Clear Who Is Responsible for What 158
28. Attaching Authority to Responsibility 164
29. Developing Useful Information That Is Readily
    Available to Everyone 171

PUTTING IT ALL TOGETHER 179

PREFACE

NINETEEN fifty-eight was a good news/bad news year for engineering graduates. There was a mild recession and companies were not hiring by the numbers ("get me ten EEs, eight MEs, and two IEs") as they had in prior years. They were much more selective and wanted engineers near the top of the class. If you had a high ranking, you got several offers at the expense of people down the list who didn't get any. In this kind of market, "pay for performance" had real meaning.

I was first in my electrical engineering class at Drexel Institute in Philadelphia and determined to negotiate a good deal. That meant finding a job with a successful electronics company that had good growth potential, a modern plant in a pleasant suburb, and paid a high salary.

Having put myself through college by working both part time and on the Drexel Co-op program (six months in school, six months in industry), my job selection criteria quickly reduced to the basics — I took the highest offer. That was $7,000 a year, more than my mother and father who worked all their lives made between them, and a sum so high that I wondered what I would do with it all (a problem I solved immediately and never had again).

The winning bidder was the research laboratories of Philco Corporation. Philco was a struggling company (they were acquired two years later by Ford in a deal whose results were aptly described by an article in *Fortune*, titled: "Henry Ford and His Electronic Can of Worms"). What's more, the labs were definitely not in a modern plant nor in the suburbs.

I started out in an old building in a seedy neighborhood in North Philadelphia. My lab was on the second floor directly above a back entrance that had the words "Philadelphia Electric Storage Battery Company" (the name of the predecessor company in the '20s) carved in stone above the doorway. A washing machine testing facility was on the third floor and occasionally our microwave test sets were blessed with water dripping through the ceiling. Not what I had in mind, but the work was fascinating and my paycheck a pleasant reminder that the grind at Drexel had been worth it.

In spite of this inelegant environment, Philco, for reasons few of us think about when picking a place to start a career, turned out to be the best choice I could have made. Undergoing a continual series of management upheavals and product reorientations, Philco was a company in flux. It was a golden opportunity for young, bright workaholics. I took part in the death and birth of a wide range of new products and technologies as I went up the management ranks — moving in behind as bodies went overboard and getting responsibilities intended for much older managers. I spent 21 years with Philco and its successors, and I packed several careers into that one generation. My force-feeding in management training at Philco became the foundation for this book.

I was taught by example what motivates people to work at the top of their potential. I was shown approaches that create effective organizations as well as approaches that consistently create paralysis. I went through case histories, showing what makes one operation more productive than another and what makes one business succeed and another fail. The years I invested at Philco were tuition for things that could not be taught in any school. And even with all the upheavals and closed businesses that were to come, there was a lot of fun in the learning.

My accelerated management course started in 1958. That year Philco was at the top in the new field of transistors. The Lansdale Tube Company, a small division in the Philadelphia suburbs, was an industry leader in the conversion from vacuum tubes to transistors. With a clear edge in germanium technology and automated production techniques, Lansdale developed assembly lines that churned out sophisticated transistors at high rates.

The boxes the transistors were shipped in had a map of the United States with concentric circles radiating out from the southeast corner of Pennsylvania over the phrase, "Transistor Center USA." It really was. When application engineers from Lansdale made field marketing trips, the regional salesman set up shop in a suite in a central hotel and the customers poured in to see *them*. It was heady stuff and the tiny Lansdale division contributed a major part of Philco's earnings per share in 1958.

That was the peak. In just five years Philco was not only no longer number one in transistors, it was out of the business. The company was trying desperately to establish a position in the new field of integrated circuits, based on silicon technology. Silicon operated at higher temperatures than germanium and had taken over the market. Techniques to process silicon were improving rapidly and the "silicon chip" revolution that would create the Silicon Valley on the West Coast was underway.

Philco, betting too long on germanium, was too late in the new market to become a serious player. They tried to leapfrog the industry by using Ford money to buy one of the Silicon Valley pioneers in metal-oxide-silicon (MOS) technology in the late '60s, but that effort was hampered by the problems of East Coast versus West Coast management (at one point the joke was that our offices were 35,000 feet over Kansas), and the semiconductor recession of 1970 – 71 was the final blow. Too late into silicon, too early into MOS, Philco withdrew from the semiconductor business in early 1971 after an unsuccessful attempt to form a joint venture with a Japanese company (a preview of the 1980s).

It was against this background that my education took place. In a period of about 15 years, Philco entered and left two of the biggest and most significant businesses of the second half of the century — the integrated circuit semiconductor business and the computer business (computers expired at a division only a few miles from Lansdale). Philco also opened and closed aerospace electronics operations covering the full spectrum of microwave and semiconductor technologies. I got to play in all of these shows, and the opening nights were marvelous (even if some of the closings were not).

The Philco name was sold with the consumer appliance business in the '70s, and my part of the company became the Ford Aerospace Corporation. I changed my role as well. After running product lines with profit and loss responsibilities and worrying about yields, contract negotiations, and marketing campaigns (how do you convince the industry that something called a backward diode is an advance in the state of the art?), I spent several years at Ford world headquarters on corporate staff (becoming for a while one of the most feared persons in industry —"help from central staff").

I got the chance to work on a "big picture" basis there, doing business planning on the billion-dollar level and making forays into international markets (a place where some third-world government officials responsible for buying major missile and communication systems encouraged marketing techniques undreamed of in the cloistered halls of Drexel).

I finished my on-the-job training by spending eight years in an entirely different set of circumstances when I left Ford Aerospace (and the winters of Detroit) and joined Hughes Aircraft Company. This gave me a chance to confirm that the key things I had learned at Philco could be considered "universal truths." I saw that what applied to a chaotic situation, filled with businesses in a constant cycle of birth and death, also applied to a much more stable, constantly growing and successful business situation like the one that prevailed in the early 1980s at Hughes.

Hughes Aircraft is a key company in the aerospace /electronics industry, and many believe it is the defense department's number one electronics contractor. In 1985, it was the object of a spirited bidding contest with General Motors and Ford as finalists. GM's eventual victory ruined the punch line for a series of jokes in my office about Ford deciding to buy me back, but I can say from a unique vantage point that GM got a better deal with Hughes than Ford did when it bought Philco a quarter century earlier.

The key attraction for me at Hughes was what appeared to be an ideal job. My assignment was to use my prior experience to develop ideas to improve productivity in what was already a successful operation, one that, for years, had won on outstanding technology, but which now had to be as innovative in cost reduction. This was an opportunity to experiment in what was for me the most interesting part of business — *how* to make operations more productive in the usually frenzied atmosphere that exists where real people do real work. The real world is driven by cost and schedule (or schedule and cost, depending on who is pushing your priority button today), and the trick is to make improvements that work in *that* environment.

That brings me to the creation of this book. I've learned what I believe are the keys to getting the best combination of productivity and quality in the working environments of the aerospace /electronics industry (and, I believe, any other industry or size of business). They're simple in concept, but that does not make them easy to implement. If it was easy, everybody would do it.

How to get improved quality and/or productivity are very popular subjects. Few subjects over the past several years have absorbed as much management attention. It's probably safe to say that every company of more than 100 people in the United States has some sort of quality and/or productivity improvement effort underway. That includes many people who are working on "Total Quality" (or a derivative thereof) with the belief that quality is what sells in today's world.

But quality, independent of costs, does not necessarily sell. You can never escape the question of whether the price is right. What *does* sell (and always has) is the proper *combination* of quality and productivity — what I have chosen to call *Productive Quality.* Productive Quality is *not* a trade-off of quality and productivity, but rather a method of operating that permits us to *simultaneously* improve quality and productivity *indefinitely.* How to do it — how to get Productive Quality — is what this book is all about.

A *Total Quality* system can be made to work because its basic concepts follow those that lead to Productive Quality. But the drill-like nature of Total Quality is not amenable to the culture of individual initiative and leadership we want in *our* work force. We get better results with less complexity by focusing on actions for Productive Quality rather than trying to install a full-blown Total Quality system.

I think the concepts distilled from my years of experience are not going to be far from what you already know or suspect to be true — work is done by people, after all, and people are much the same everywhere. But the "how" of translating those concepts into meaningful actions contains much that is new. The emphasis is on actions within your control — actions you can do with reasonable expectation that they will succeed in the environment you work in every day. They are actions that bring results.

A NOTE ON APPLYING
PRODUCTIVE QUALITY "UNIVERSALLY"

The preface discusses the "universal truths," which I found applied to quite different circumstances at Philco and Hughes. Doing the Whole Job (see page 92) discusses a "universal" job description (satisfy your customers and develop a good working relationship with your suppliers) that applies to *every* job — even if your "company" consists of one person. Similarly, the techniques discussed in the rest of the book can be applied to every size company and circumstance. The steps to get Productive Quality are universally applicable.

Many examples used in the book reflect my experience in a big company. But even if the specifics of the example are different from your circumstances, the concepts are not. Words such as "systems" and "processes" do not mean only large systems or complex processes. I worked part time at a small newspaper for many years. Delivering a paper route is a process that is part of a distribution system in the same way designing a "black box" is a process that is part of a complex communication system. If I had applied the techniques described in this book to my paper route, I would have done it faster while collecting more incentive bonuses for fewer "misses" and "spoils."

The examples in the book from the sports world show convincingly the universal applicability of the techniques to get Productive Quality. I urge you to think about how the examples can apply to your business, no matter how different. *You* know better than anyone else what the key problems are in *your* business. The thrust of this book is that Productive Quality is *not* created by copying Japanese systems or using some specific management style. What makes the difference between success and failure is the way workers are acquired and permitted to do what needs to be done. Utilizing people — including yourself — in an optimum way is the key. This book shows you *how* to do that.

WHAT TO DO
AND HOW TO PLAN
TO DO IT

CHAPTER I

SETTING THE STAGE

M ANAGEMENT performance is the key to Productive Quality.
Management performance determines whether the company
succeeds or fails. No matter how dedicated the work force or how
outstanding the product line, a poorly managed company will not
survive (a poorly managed company will have neither a dedicated
work force nor an outstanding product line for long). It's the leadership (or lack of it) by the top 10% of the people in the company that
largely determines the fate of the other 90%. The leverage is immense.

The management process works best when *everyone* in the work
force understands what they are trying to do. But that work force
must consist of competent people trying to do their jobs in an intelligent way and looking for techniques to help them do things better.
That's the kind of work force to surround yourself with (more on
that in Section II) and direct your actions toward. Plan your actions
and judge the probability of their success in that context.

With such a work force there can be discussion — not a handing
down of directions from on high. Ideally, everyone will think about
what they are doing in terms of the ideas under discussion and consider changes that might lead to a better way *for them* to do things.
Each person is the best judge of what will work and will not work in
their specific situation. They know best how to implement actions
for change. Thus, your intention is to offer ideas for discussion, not
edicts for implementation.

A few words about this book's organization and sequence: Section
I describes *what* to do (there are three basic steps to Productive
Quality) and outlines a process for doing it. This section contains the
management philosophy the process is based on and includes the key

concepts of two associated subjects — Total Quality (TQ) and Measures. Although trying to implement a full-blown TQ system is probably *not* a good idea for most companies (see A Total Quality Sampler, page 25), the concepts discussed in the TQ and Measures chapters are integral to understanding the process of achieving Productive Quality.

The other three sections of the book discuss in detail *how* you can take the three steps to Productive Quality. There is a separate section for each step, and these sections form the bulk of the book. *How* to get Productive Quality concerns most of the book. But knowing *what* to do has to be first.

CHAPTER 2

WHAT YOU ARE
TRYING TO DO

WHAT VERSUS HOW

As a manager, you have to decide *what* you want to do before starting on the *how*. You want to be sure that everyone is trying to solve the same problem or achieve the same goal. Defining exactly what you're trying to accomplish before getting to the question of how best to do it saves a lot of time and effort.

THE BASIC PREMISE

No management approach or system can guarantee success in all organizations under all conditions. Organizations operate under different constraints in different environments, and no one management system will work for all. In fact, the same organization undergoes constant changes in operating constraints and environments, and systems that were appropriate before may no longer apply.

You can look at the systems a successful company used to get where it is today, but often that's an exercise in preparing to fight the previous war. The company you are studying may have already changed its approach due to changing conditions; or, as often happens, the successful example ceases to be successful because as conditions change, it continues to follow the same operating system.

Sports offer good examples of this premise. The football team that succeeded on "three yards and a cloud of dust" starts getting beaten regularly by passing teams. The baseball team that won so long with speed and defense starts losing to a barrage of three-run homers. The basketball team that depended on leading the league in rebounds and bruises is run over by the trend to fast-break. Or vice versa in all three cases. What *is* the best approach?

The answer is provided by teams that win with different approaches in different circumstances. They have no "best" approach. Their approach is based on the talent of the available players. Lots of muscle means it's three-run homer time. The decade's best point guard and some runners and gunners go to the fast break. When the best long passer emerges at camp, add some sprinters and go with the mad bomber offense. Any of these approaches can — and do — win it all. But none of them can win without good players.

That brings us to the core of my basic premise. *The key is the players, not the system.* No system can be made to work well without good players. But, any reasonable system applied consistently can be made to work well with good players. Clearly, some systems fit certain players better than others, but it's much easier to find a system to fit good players than it is to find good players to fit a system. Talent is the unique commodity, and you must take it in whatever form it is available. Systems can be changed easily.

The one constant in successful companies is the performance and /or new ideas of a few key people. If new ideas aren't added continually, success disappears. You can't necessarily copy the ideas because they may not apply to your situation, no matter how much you try to make them fit. What you can emulate is getting people who consistently give the ideas and /or performance that you need in *your* situation.

WHAT TO DO?

Based on this premise, what you need to do can be stated in three sentences. These three sentences — or three steps — are the distillation of 30 years of experience. As you'll see, many people have come to the same conclusions over the last century. The three steps to take are:

1. Get and keep only the best people.

2. Make clear to them what needs to be done — define the job in terms of what is considered good performance and what results are expected.

3. Let them do it — create conditions in which they can do what needs to be done.

That's it. Like most apparently simple approaches, it works very well but, in fact, demands a lot of hard work to make it succeed. There still is no free lunch. You'll learn *how* to put these steps into practice in the last three sections of the book. First there is a sanity check to see why a lot of other people came to the same conclusions.

NOTHING IS NEW
UNDER THE SUN — MAYBE

In his book published in 1911 titled *The Principles of Scientific Management*, Frederick W. Taylor stated that a new approach to management was needed to bring rational and scientific practices into the work place. His four principles of scientific management, paraphrased and arranged in the order of my three statements, were:

1. Carefully select workers who have the ability to do the job.

2. Develop a scientific approach for every job, which includes rules of motion, standard tools, and appropriate working conditions.

3. Carefully train the selected workers to do the job and provide incentives for them to cooperate with the scientific approach.

4. Support the workers by planning carefully how the work is to be done and by "smoothing" the way for them to do their jobs. (Subsequently, Taylor said this step usually was done inadequately because managers felt (1) it was "too much trouble" and (2) they must be perceived as doing at least 50% of the work. Section IV tells how to avoid these problems.)

7

Paraphrasing Taylor a little, you have: Get the right people; make clear what needs to be done, and make the appropriate training available; create conditions under which they can do what needs to be done. This was the revolution of 1911.

Let's fast-forward to Japan in the early 1950s. With survival as the incentive, American quality consultants W. Edwards Deming and J. M. Juran were invited to Japan to discuss how to adapt Western methods to help rebuild Japan's economy. (Their fame in the United States in the 1980s was due to the credit the Japanese gave them for Japan's worldwide economic success.) Deming (after whom the Japanese Deming Prize for quality is named) taught them how to use statistical process control to improve quality while Juran showed how to involve all layers of management in the quality improvement process. The Japanese concluded that the implementation of Taylor's ideas had evolved into rigidly defined jobs that workers executed on order. Improvements to the system came primarily from designers of the system, not from the people who worked within it. This method of quality control failed to take advantage of a recent twentieth-century resource that was uniquely well developed in Japan — a pool of people who were fully literate and well educated. Such people could do much more than act as a clever piece of machinery (Taylor probably would have agreed enthusiastically).

Deming and Juran provided the tools such people could use to improve systems. The Japanese set out to improve the way the Taylor approach had been implemented by adapting these ideas to fit their environment. Over the next 15 years, they evolved the system we call Total Quality. They ended up with products that have the best Productive Quality on a worldwide basis. But the keys to their approach (see A Total Quality Sampler, page 25) were exactly the same three steps listed previously.

They invested their resources in selecting an elite work force (and I use the word "elite" deliberately). They screened workers carefully for both assembly line and professional jobs. They established contacts with selected schools to direct the best applicants to their companies, and they set up testing and training programs for people *before* they were hired. They hired only those people who would work well in the conditions they planned to create. Essentially, this is finding talent to fit an existing system, and one aspect of Total Quality that can be improved upon by using a different approach in the United States. But it is clearly getting and keeping only the best people.

This process was used to staff the GM/Toyota venture called NUMMI (New United Motors Manufacturing, Inc. in Fremont, California), where workers from the previous GM operation underwent a three-day screening process before they were considered for hiring. What's more, new candidates were interviewed and hired (or rejected) by the same teams they were going to work with. More recently, Ford Motor Company announced in May 1988 that they were hiring new workers for the first time since the layoffs of the early '80s and that they were going to use much more "intensive" screening, testing, and interviewing methods (learned from "foreign" auto makers who have factories in the United States). They used to hire a worker on Friday to start on Monday, but now the hiring process can take as much as a month. Get and keep only the best is an idea whose time has obviously arrived.

The Japanese follow up their careful hiring program with continual training and indoctrination (even in the new Mazda plant opened in Flat Rock, Michigan, in 1987, newly hired workers — who made up only 4% of those who had applied — "participated in a rigorous 10-week training course followed by off-line training with a team leader"). As a result, there is no doubt in any worker's mind about what he or she is expected to do and *how* they are expected to go about their work. Reminders are continuous — education is part of the success of the Total Quality system.) The bottom line of this educational process is that workers learn they are expected to create ways to continually improve the system. That is the key part of their jobs. They know explicitly how to *operate*, not just what task to per-

9

form — and this applies to all "workers," marketing managers as well as assembly line workers. It is a total education process.

The Japanese then created a system in which workers can do exactly what they have been trained to do. Teams called quality circles are "voluntarily" formed to work on system problems. (They are voluntary only in the sense that no one is ordered to join — but anyone not willing to join was not hired in the first place.) People feel *permitted* to contribute as well *expected* to contribute because the system was designed to change based on their input. Total Quality works for the Japanese because what is expected is clear to everyone and only those who can meet those expectations are hired.

The short form of Total Quality becomes: Get and keep only the best people; make clear to them what needs to be done; and create conditions in which they can do it. Seventy-five years after Taylor's revolution, the same thing is still being said — but with a distinctly new flavor. Now the improvements to the system come primarily from the people who work in the system and, therefore, know it best.

THE GOOD OLD DAYS

Forget about Taylor and the Japanese, and draw some conclusions from your own experience. I believe you'll find the same answers they did. Think of the times you've sat in soul-searching meetings addressing the problems of how to improve or be more productive or be more competitive. Flip charts or blackboards (or whiteboards) are filled with lists of key issues. What shows up in the first position? — getting/ keeping the best (or better) people. It happens every time. It's like the advice "buy low, sell high"; the difference here is that you're going to learn *how* to do it.

Think back to your own "good old days." There have been times when, compared to today, you've operated in poor facilities, had primitive tools, worked under intense schedule and cost pressures (do it or close up shop is pressure of the first order), and the job still got done. In fact, you were never more productive. You didn't operate under some specific theory of organization, some complicated merit compensation plan, or need to hold meetings to talk about how to be more productive. You just did what had to be done and did it productively (in terms of getting it shipped with what was at hand).

Be careful about looking back too fondly at such times because part of the nostalgia is tinged with having been younger and more innocent. Most would rebel if asked to work under such conditions tomorrow morning. But remember the key things. There were good people (you knew how to get a task force — cherry pick the best people from each area). They knew exactly what to do and what was expected in the broadest possible terms — the job was not just to build or test or rework — the job was to do whatever it took to complete it on time. Any necessary training was available, you knew the expected results, and there was an organization in which it was possible to succeed. You had the authority you needed and the responsibility for making decisions; people responded when something was requested — the system was set up to support you.

Many will recognize this as essentially "crisis management" — not something to recommend doing on a regular basis. But it *is* worthwhile to think about what solved a problem when "in extremis" — if the *basic* elements could be accomplished on a regular basis, maybe "extremis" could be avoided in the first place.

The basics of your productivity were:

1. You got the best people.

2. You made clear what needed to be done and made clear how everyone was expected to perform as part of the team.

3. The authority that was needed was given, existing systems were modified to fit, and the leaders led until they asked for help.

Sound familiar? Get good people, make clear what needs to be done, and let them do it. Organizations in start-up situations that make something out of nothing and organizations that succeed relentlessly every year in bigger and better ways carry out precisely these same three steps.

11

IF WE'RE SO SMART,
WHY AREN'T WE RICH?

Others who have agreed with the three steps include the first John D. Rockefeller, who said in the 1880s that the secret to success was to "find the man who can do the particular thing you need done and then leave him alone to do it unhampered." A generation later Teddy Roosevelt said that "the best executive is the one who has sense enough to pick good men to do what he wants done, and self-restraint enough to keep from meddling with them while they do it." The three steps clearly are not a new thought. But if these steps are so basic, and they've been known for such a long time, then the obvious question is why doesn't everyone do them?

The answer is that they are very hard to follow in our normal environment. As I said, "buy low, sell high" has been standard advice for a long time, too, and no one will argue that it doesn't work. The key is knowing *how* to do it. The reason everyone doesn't implement the three steps is that it's not clear *how* to do them while buried under the hundreds of nagging problems each of us has to deal with every day at work.

How do you put these steps into action while still getting shipments out at the end of the month, programs done on time and within budget, going to meetings to report on situations that have not changed because of time spent in other meetings reporting on and /or discovering the status of other problems? In short, doing all the things that are part of everyday survival?

The three steps *can* be done while struggling with day-to-day problems by taking the actions outlined in this book. Some require changing the way you think about your job and responsibilities. You may find you are already taking some of these actions, but with limited impact because other key actions are not done. But all the actions have two things in common: Their implementation is within *your* control, and they all *do* work.

The distinction between what does work and what should work is very important. Your actions have been selected from years of experience using that key filter — does it work? There are many behavioral and management theories that should work. But many of them don't work in the real world where the work is being done. Only things that work are in your list of actions. Things that *should* work are irrelevant.

CHAPTER 3

A MANAGEMENT PHILOSOPHY

W*HAT* to do has been discussed; the rest of this book is about *how* to do it. Let's talk about the "management philosophy" — or framework—you need to do the three steps (get and keep only the best people, make clear what needs to be done, and let them do it). Understanding the framework helps you react to change and adjust your actions to fit new situations.

Just as "20 key goals" is a contradiction in terms (they can't all be "key" if there are 20 of them — 5 perhaps, but not 20), the number of tenets in a *useable* framework must be small. Here there are two. Everything that follows is built on these two — and on the foundation of doing only what works. The two tenets are:

1. Doing things a little bit at a time, all the time, has the highest probability of success.

2. Leading beats managing.

What do each of these mean and how do you do them?

A DIFFERENT APPROACH
TO THE FORCED MARCH

Most of what is done daily is a forced march. You try to balance your time between reacting to today's new problems and keeping previous commitments. Priorities are set by problems that have to be addressed *now* — in manufacturing, many of those priorities are products that have to be shipped *now* and/or new bids that have to be made *now*. No matter how hard you try to manage time wisely, there is little extra time to apply to things such as the three steps. Any actions to implement them can be postponed for today, and that postponement can turn into years — one day at a time. You work in the real world, and that's how the real world works.

People anxious to do something about issues such as the three steps often try to use one of two techniques — what I call the *crash program* and the *grand design*. These techniques do not work in implementing constant and consistent Productive Quality. A large amount of product can be shipped in a short time with a crash program. A good facilities plan can be developed with the grand design technique. But both are temporary measures and cannot turn the three steps into a reality.

A technique does exist for addressing such issues while on the forced march of everyday work. It's based on action *now* in small increments. Thinking this way also helps you take advantage of unexpected work breaks (delayed input from others, postponed or short meetings) that add up to substantial increments of time. If used consistently, substantial pieces of work can be accomplished. It's what I call the *A Little Bit At A Time All The Time* technique. It works well for just about anything, but it is especially well suited to address the problem of the forced march.

A LITTLE BIT AT A TIME ALL THE TIME

A little bit at a time defines a mindset and a method of attacking problems of the type in this book. The mindset is that you don't have to create a big block of time or an extensive campaign to get something useful started. Some useful work can be done today, no matter how little time is assigned. That piece of work will suggest another useful action — yours or someone else's — and doing this consistently will lead to real progress. It *does* take time to solve long-standing problems, but the amount of time can be minimized by starting now. It's the difference between *doing* something and *planning* to do something "when we have time." It's a prescription for making change actually happen.

As a method of attack, *a little bit at a time all the time* means identifying pieces of the problem that can be controlled individually. Pick a piece to start on *right now*, and do something on *some* piece every day. Be aggressive (start right *now*), hard nosed (progress *every* day), persistent (stay on a problem until there is improvement), and flexible (you can do lot of pieces in parallel when done a piece at a time).

The meaning of "a little bit" does not imply that you make progress slowly. The expectation is to run consistently at a higher real percentage of completion than any crash program or grand design. Starting *now* helps people do things with the perception that there's time to "do it right." That gets them to think about approaches they wouldn't consider in a fire-fighting atmosphere. Working this way has the greatest probability of success. You get credibility from accepting that success is not going to happen immediately; insight comes from identifying pieces of a problem people can control individually; and the iterative process works because an environment of learning by doing is created, encouraging people *in* the process to recommend changes.

THE PRINCIPLE OF
PERSISTENT PROBABILITY

Both parts of a little bit at a time all the time are important. Learning how to divide a problem into the proper pieces is only the first step — you have to learn how to make progress *all* the time. When you do both parts, the principle of persistent probability is brought into play.

All any managerial approach can offer is to continually increase the probability of success in getting the job done. No *single* thing can be done to succeed — it takes a thousand small things *all* done well. If things that increase the probability of success are done *every* day, the accumulative effort will produce dramatic results. But it follows an exponential curve, and effort has to be put into it persistently. If you quit too soon because there are no immediate results and then start over again, you never arrive at the point of rapid, accumulative growth. It's an iterative, cumulative process and many things have to be worked in parallel — *a little bit at a time all the time.*

This approach requires a lot of persistence. But "he who persists wins" — if he or she persists at the right things. Making the same mistake repeatedly is undesirable no matter what it's called — unfortunately many people call it experience. If adjustments are made so the probability of success is persistently improved, ultimately you will succeed.

A LITTLE BIT AT A TIME ALL THE TIME — FIVE KEYS FOR SUCCESS

There are five keys to doing a little bit at a time all the time.

Any amount of effort is worthwhile if it is done all the time. Do something today even if there's not enough time to do it "justice." As little as fifteen minutes a day produces an accumulation of effort, and the wheel does not have to be reinvented every time you begin. No effort is too small if applied consistently. Failing to start now because "there's not enough time" permits months to go by in which nothing happens to improve a situation.

Learn by doing. Start now with an action or a direction and do it consistently; you will learn in a short time what really needs to be done. Rarely is it what was thought at the beginning. Working on a problem triggers new ideas as a result of the iterative process. This doesn't happen if you wait for a "detailed plan" before beginning. There is nothing wrong with making a plan, but you don't need it to take a first step. That step begins the iterative process and helps an intelligent plan evolve.

Start simple. Don't sink a good idea by weighting it down. Getting together, talking about a problem, and developing a feeling for what needs to be done is all that's required to start a useful process. There's no need for a lot of preparation, home-work, actions, and agendas, especially if starting is delayed until all of that is ready. Similarly, a "what if" analysis done at a macro level with whatever data is available is often all you need to decide what needs to be done *next*. Doing *now* what *can* be done *now* gets the process started.

No improvement is too small to implement. A single day's compound interest is not impressive in terms of the amount of interest added — it's the cumulative effect that makes your IRA grow. *Continually* make improvements, no matter how small. Complex systems (that work) are built (and fine tuned) one step at a time. You never know which small fix may lead to improvements in other problems thought to be unrelated.

There is no end point to the process. This is definitely a "what have you done for me lately?" process. *Continually* im-prove—*all* the time. Don't use crash programs to improve the yield — expect improvements *all* the time — no level is "good enough." (This is the essence of the Japanese word "kaizen" — dogged improvement *all* the time.) It sounds tough — but it's a tough process (if it was easy to do, everybody would do it). Do it a little bit at a time, *all* the time — until you retire. Then some-one else keeps doing it until they retire. It's a long-term invest-ment that yields a higher return on the time invested than any other approach.

THE NEED FOR WORKING A LITTLE BIT AT A TIME

Action lists for issues such as "productivity improvement," "reten-tion of key people," or "working smarter" reappear every year. These are complex problems with complex solutions that will not yield to short-term attacks. One meeting or a series of meetings over a fixed period of time will not do. Everyone is too busy with the regular workday to undertake the major effort that's needed to solve "big" problems immediately. These problems have many interconnections, making it nearly impossible to assign one person or group to push solutions through all the paths involved and expect long-lived results.

Cut the problems into pieces and address them separately. The pieces have to be small enough for one person to take actions on the piece that is under their control. This is done with any major program. No one person builds a complicated weapons system or figures out how to put a man on the moon. The project is cut into pieces; each person gets a piece they can do, and when finished goes on to the next piece. Thousands of people working persistently on thousands of pieces make a big thing happen.

If the "pieces" approach is adopted without a second thought on a large program, why not do it to change the way you manage, hire, train, or assign authority? The big inhibitor is the perception of the time it should take to solve these problems. Ten years to put a man on the moon is accepted easily. But when the call comes for "improved productivity," "safety first," or "better quality" it's difficult for people to accept that the solution requires a series of steps that will take years to complete (not to mention the need to continue specific actions forever).

When the boss raises his voice about a problem that has happened *again*, and it's clearly due to a system that simply doesn't work, and he asks when the problem is going to be fixed *for good*, can you imagine telling him that you know exactly how to fix the problem and will have it done in two years? It takes a lot of courage to avoid promising to fix it by next month. Two years sounds like forever.

But two years will pass no matter how many actions are taken — or not taken. If the problem is not addressed in small pieces that can be conquered one piece at a time, the problem will still be there in two years — and the two after that. If the pieces are defined so that solving them is in your realm of control, they will be manageable within the regular workday. Finding out what aspect of the problem you can pull away from the whole and can work on independently is a valuable process; it's surprising how much can be done without waiting for "them" to do something. And if you process those pieces on your own persistently, you will make progress *a little bit at a time all the time.*

CRASH PROGRAMS (THAT CRASH) AND GRAND DESIGNS (THAT ARE TOO GRAND)

The crash program is a call to arms for a group of people to solve a problem in a hurry. But the problems we are concerned with do not yield permanently to this approach. The pressures of the workday and the frustration of seeing how much time and effort it will take to implement lasting changes result in the crash program, which fades in proportion to the fading of the crisis atmosphere. Good short-term results can be accomplished by crash programs, but problems will return because they were never really solved. Products can be shipped in a hurry with a crash program, and when shipping is done, the problem that needed immediate attention is solved. But the problem that originated the need for the crash program wasn't solved, and you will need crash programs again and again — each one more expensive than the one before.

It's like an annual crash diet — the result is an honest effort that removes weight. But if the old diet produced the weight problem, the weight problem will return when the crash diet ends. A permanent dietary change that cuts about 125 calories a day (three cookies) will remove over ten pounds a year. Cutting the equivalent number of calories from other small selections will cause further annual weight loss, resulting in permanent weight loss from a permanent diet change (a little bit at a time all the time . . .).

The other end of the spectrum — the grand design — filled with milestones, detailed action plans, micromeasures, committee meetings, and progress reports, doesn't work for either "productivity improvement" or solving immediate problems. First, you don't know what works well until you try it. Second, people perceive they are already too busy; signing up for a "grand design" program (in addition to what they are doing) does not seem possible, even if they would like to try. It's just another burden.

Such programs often don't get beyond the introduction phase. In a series of initial meetings, problems are discussed in an intelligent way and solutions outlined. But the meetings tend to run on indefinitely, and dismay grows as the paperwork grows. A lot of good ideas die waiting for all the interconnections to be made. The number of required conditions before ideas are implemented seems limitless and the time required to meet them appears to extend beyond the normal life span.

The crash program happens fast (by edict), but it won't solve the root cause of the problem — only the present symptom will be corrected. The grand design could solve the root cause of the problem but often doesn't get launched — and if it does, can't be sustained. Doing a little bit at a time all the time gets you started *now* and begins a process that can be *sustained.* It maximizes the probability of success — and that's all that can be asked of any managerial process.

Remember the two tenets in management philosophy: Doing things a little bit at a time all the time has the highest probability of success; and leading beats managing. The next chapter addresses the second tenet, which has been said many times, but it works best when moving ahead a little bit at a time all the time. Each tenet complements the other and gives a framework that you can use successfully.

CHAPTER 4

WHY LEADING BEATS MANAGING

LEADING rather than managing has emerged as a popular idea over the past decade, but it is not always clear what a "leader" is expected to do compared to what a "manager" does. This section will discuss what is meant by leading versus managing as well as how to lead. Leading is better than managing for two reasons: (1) Leading has a higher probability of getting the performance you want from people. (2) Leading gives you the maximum amount of time for the things only you can do — your concentration on *those* things maximizes the probability of success.

WHAT DOES A LEADER DO VERSUS A MANAGER?

The difference between a leader and a manager is shown by the work they choose to do. A leader focuses on creating an operation that will handle any task effectively in the manner he or she wants. (This is part of what some people call having a "vision" or "mission" for the operation). A manager focuses on doing the assigned tasks effectively. He or she guides and helps people in those tasks, performing some of them when the situation demands it. A leader focuses on getting the best people, making clear what needs to be done, and making it possible for them to do what needs to be done. Completing the tasks is the responsibility of the work force.

To better understand leading versus managing, think about the old saying: "When you give a man a fish you feed him for a day; when you teach him how to fish you feed him for a lifetime." Let's build on that idea and assume the job is to get fish from the river. You hire people, teach them how to catch fish, provide them with fishing tackle, and they go after the fish.

A manager — who often gets the job by being the best at fishing in the area — concentrates on helping each person catch as many fish as possible. When times are tight, the manager fishes. The focus is on fishing. A leader concentrates on recruiting the best fishermen in the area, providing good fishing tackle and data on where the fish are, and keeping the river clean and capable of supporting fish. Leaders talk to people to find out what is needed in these areas so they can catch more fish. The one thing leaders do not do is fish; they depend on the work force to do that. The work force focuses its energies on developing the best ways to fish — they are in control of the fishing. In fact, leaders may be lousy fishermen. But the time not spent fishing or helping people fish permits them to work on the other problems. If he or she is as good a leader as the manager is a manager, the leader's team will catch more fish and will increase the yield continually.

There is no *one* thing a leader does as opposed to a manager. The choice between leading and managing is something done in a thousand small acts. It's the selection of daily actions you can take as part of your job. Your job as leader is to get and keep only the best people, to make clear what needs to be done, and to let them do it. The first part is the most important, but the daily basis of leadership comes from handling the last two parts. Avoid the temptation to get too involved in helping people do *their* jobs. Getting their jobs done is not your job. Your job is to make it possible for them to do their jobs.

You are attempting to create an atmosphere of job ownership. People should feel they own their jobs and have the responsibility — and the authority — to improve continually the way their jobs are done. This drives Productive Quality. No one can recommend job improvements better than the person who is doing the job. But they need to know that recommending improvements is part of their job, to understand that nothing is off limits, and to believe that changes can actually result from their recommendations. If you give them that kind of leadership, you will get the results you want.

HOW DO YOU LEAD
RATHER THAN MANAGE?

Leadership includes all the things that are outlined in the chapters to come. But in terms of making decisions against the framework, you have to remind yourself about *your* job and mission for the operation. Then, among alternative actions, choose those that make it possible for people to do their jobs in the way those jobs need to be done. If you do that every day (a little bit at a time, all the time), you will be leading and leading well.

Now that you understand what you are trying to do and have a framework for doing it, some concepts need to be added. These concepts, to which you will refer when you get to the nitty-gritty of how to implement the three steps, are included in the next two chapters about Total Quality and Measures.

CHAPTER 5

A TOTAL QUALITY SAMPLER

THE CAVEATS

TOTAL QUALITY (TQ) is built on the three steps: Get and keep only the best people; make clear what needs to be done; let them do it. We can consider the fact that TQ has been very successful in Japan as a litmus test, demonstrating that a management approach built on the these steps will succeed. Any reasonable management approach built on the steps will succeed — it's the three steps that are the key to success, not the management approach. TQ in its purest form is not implemented easily and requires a degree of structure and regimentation that may be counterproductive in a culture that gives its highest awards for personal initiative and willingness to try something different. TQ *does* work, but the substantial investments of time and energy to make it work would yield a better return if directed towards doing the three steps within the simplest management approach.

However, many elements of TQ are consistent with the way you want people to operate in *any* system. These elements play an important part in *how* to do the three steps. Thus, it's useful to understand what TQ consists of and how it is done. Then you will understand the concepts I've adapted and see more clearly how they can give the results you want.

THE BASICS OF TOTAL QUALITY

TQ stresses individual responsibility for quality. Everyone is expected to improve the process used to perform their job continually so that variation is always being reduced. This improves productivity and quality simultaneously (leading to Productive Quality). "Everyone" means everyone — not just manufacturing. (This emphasis on including all of the company's activities led the Japanese to call the approach "Company-Wide Quality Control".)

This *simultaneous* improvement of productivity (better cost and delivery) and quality (better customer satisfaction) is TQ's prime benefit. It's not just better quality in terms of performance — customer satisfaction means a combination of performance, cost, and delivery. In addition, the purpose of TQ is not to build better morale or teamwork or company spirit. Those things are benefits of the process. The bottom line is that if TQ did not result in Productive Quality, no one (including the Japanese) would implement it.

It is the ongoing emphasis on reduction of variation in *all* processes that makes TQ work. Rework, scrap, inventories and the resources needed to service them, engineering lead times, and overhead and capital investment are reduced. Fewer direct *and* indirect people are needed to produce a given level of output, and — simultaneously — the product the customer receives has less and less variation, which improves the performance /cost ratio. This increases market share, which permits another round of cost reduction. Productive Quality always sells.

What's new in TQ is:

1. Individuals are responsible for the quality of what they produce — whether it is a product or a service.

2. Part of each person's job is to improve the process they use continually, not just perform a task in the process.

3. Everyone in the company is expected to understand TQ (an immense educational task).

4. The company's systems must be designed to support the continual improvement of those systems by the people who work in the system.

The basic principle is that if everyone improves their individual job continually, the company as a whole continually improves its competitive position.

Note the emphasis on *individual* responsibility in TQ. This is a key concept. There's a misperception that *the* key ingredient of TQ is teamwork. This is incorrect. Teamwork is *an* important ingredient — as it is in every human endeavor where the output is the result of more than one person. Teamwork is the way to get the most out of your players, and team output should always take precedence over individual output if the two conflict. But all the team organization in the world won't achieve Productive Quality — or the most wins — if the individuals on the team do not understand their role and /or are not *capable* of performing that role. Focus on good teamwork *after* you get the best players, make clear what needs to be done, and make it possible for it to be done. If TQ team members are not capable of proposing improvements, and /or nothing changes when they do propose improvements, then teamwork is meaningless.

It took the Japanese about 20 years of trial and error to evolve their system, and they are still making changes. It takes three to five years to implement a working model from scratch, even when a basic plan is known in advance. It is, in short, very difficult to do — that's why companies able to do it have a competitive edge (but any company capable of installing a TQ system is also capable of doing the three steps consistently and that's where the edge comes from).

THE DETAILS OF TOTAL QUALITY

Now that the basics of TQ have been defined, let's look at the operating concepts involved. Although simultaneous improvement of productivity and quality may sound too good to be true, it is a given if the same key drivers apply to both. You improve both productivity and quality when you improve those key drivers.

Understanding the drivers for TQ requires understanding the use of the word "quality." A quality product or service satisfies the needs of the customer. This definition requires that you understand the customer's needs. You have no other way to be sure that you are providing quality products and services. This requires you to know who your customer is, talk with them to know when their needs change

27

and to predict unexpressed future needs, and find a way to measure your ability to meet their needs so that ability can be improved continually.

The customer you are concerned with is the individual customer, who is the next person in the process. That means the next person on the assembly line, the next section to which the product is delivered, the next department, the next division, and, ultimately, the person who buys the company's products. That final buyer is satisfied with the company only when you satisfy each preceding individual customer.

As everyone has at least one customer, they have at least one supplier — the person prior to them in the process. You can go through the company chain (in the opposite direction you went for customers) and ultimately reach a supplier outside the company. However, for most people, suppliers *and* customers are inside the company. Since everyone is both a customer and supplier, all have the same job: Satisfy the customer and develop a good working relationship with the supplier. If this is done well individually by everyone in the company, then it is done well as a company. That is the crux of TQ.

HOW DO YOU DO IT?

Satisfy customers by continually improving the job for that customer. Continual improvement is done by collecting data and measuring whether the process gets better when changes are made. Use the data initially to bring the process under control, then make changes that improve it. The process can't be improved if it is not measured. Job knowledge and job measures are needed.

Job knowledge means to go beyond learning just the mechanics of your job. Learn to understand the systems and processes used to do your job. Job knowledge is acquired by applying job measures, and the ability to apply job measures is acquired by education in the process of measurement (the same way you are educated in the overall process of TQ). The Japanese say that TQ begins and ends with education. To implement TQ everyone must understand what they are supposed to do, how to do it, and be permitted to do it.

TOTAL QUALITY, THE THREE STEPS, AND MANAGEMENT PHILOSOPHY

A Japanese word applied to TQ has become familiar to many Western companies. The word is *kaizen*. It does not have an exact equivalent in English, but means continual improvement in a series of small incremental steps. If one practices kaizen, one advances TQ and achieves an output with Productive Quality.

It's a small step from kaizen to a little bit at a time all the time. Also, management emphasis in TQ is on developing systems that support the people doing the work — the essence of leading rather than managing. Thus, as well as implementing the three steps, TQ is based on the same management philosophy as Productive Quality.

Achieving TQ or Productive Quality is accomplished by doing many of the same things. As you will see, several of the actions taken to implement the three steps in Productive Quality are similar to what you have gone through in this sampler. It's a result of working from the same basic management philosophy. But you don't need a lot of the "trappings" of TQ (especially the endless audits) to get the results you want. By doing the basic things right, positive results follow without the extra layers of organizational structure that usually accompany TQ. The rest of the book shows *how* to do the basic things "right."

CHAPTER 6

A MEASURES PRIMER

THE CAVEATS ONCE AGAIN

THERE may be more wasted energy put into measures than into any other effort in industry today. Three-ring binders whose only real utility is filling bookshelves are full of measures. Measures can become little more than the lead act in a dog and pony show for management. Bad decisions based on the improper use of measures can incur substantial costs. Understand *what* you are trying to *do* when measuring. What to measure is not the big issue (that is learned by measuring), but knowing what to *do* with the measure is everything.

WHAT TO DO WITH MEASURES

This primer focuses on two main uses of measures: Getting organizational results by measuring individual results, and continual improvement through reduced variation.

Individual measures determine continual improvement in individual performance and the capability of the processes that are used. Final organizational results are an accumulation of individual results. Final results are the most important measure because they determine whether the business remains open. Final results are improved by focusing on individual results; only at the individual level is there a direct connection between cause and effect.

People can be expected to improve — and be responsible for — only what is under their individual control. The person who controls the resources used in a series of processes can be measured on the final result of those processes. The person who controls one process also needs a measure at that level to see what effect their changes have on how well they do. As individual results improve, the entire process or series of processes improves. To improve the final result, improve the series of individual results.

THE ABNER DOUBLEDAY ANALOGY

Consider a baseball team. The final result is the maximum number of wins. No one player controls that result. The manager is held responsible for wins. If the team doesn't win as many games as it should, he is fired. He understands that criteria. Every manager lasts only until wins fall to a level that causes him to be fired. It's part of the job description. But the players are judged by individual measures. They make the team succeed by doing their individual jobs well.

Hitters can use measures such as runs produced, total average, batting average, home runs, and runs batted in. Pitchers have earned run average, innings pitched per start, strike/ball ratios, and saves. Which measure to use depends on the role assigned to the player. Power hitters can hit almost any average and still be the most valuable player if they hit enough home runs and drive in enough runs. Single hitters should have high on-base averages and score lots of runs. Starting pitchers should get into the late innings without yielding more than three to four earned runs. Relief pitchers should have a high percentage of saves.

All of these measures are basically within the control of the individual player and can be used to measure individual performance. Not a single measure is tied to wins. You can't add up batting averages and get wins. But if every player gets the individual results expected, the probability is high that they will get the maximum number of wins. If every player increases his individual performance continually, then the probability of winning increases continually. That's the best to expect from any measurement system, and that's how to measure.

Individuals can use measures at several levels. Where training correlates with individual performance, the extent of training can be measured. Hours and pounds and repetitions in the weight room, hours and miles of running, and hours hitting against the pitching machine. All of these measures are under the control of individual players and continual improvement is their responsibility. Dividing processes into ever smaller pieces to get those that are controlled individually is how to get measures that can be used in a meaningful way.

The team understands that the purpose is to win. No measure affects the well-being of everyone on the team as greatly as the number of wins. That's the output of the team. Everyone should spend a lot of energy thinking of ways they can help the team win. If there are not enough wins, there's no play-off money, and, ultimately, not enough revenue from all sources and everyone suffers. The incentives to win are strong, and if the situation arises, an individual player is expected to take an action to improve the final result (wins) even if it comes at the expense of his individual results. That's the true definition of teamwork. But what measures get more wins? Measure the things controlled individually. Then, continually improve those things. If all members participate, the team gets better; wins increase, and so does revenue.

Note that team management — whose jobs are tied most directly to wins — do not play the game at all. They focus on getting and keeping only the best players, making clear what needs to be done, and making it possible for players to do it. (This includes providing training, supplies, good travel arrangements, good park conditions, and a system that blends the talents of the team properly.) They maximize the number of wins by making it possible for players to succeed and by measuring what those players are responsible for individually. The managers measure *their* success by wins, but they understand cause and effect.

FROM ABNER DOUBLEDAY TO EVERYDAY — LEARNING TO MEASURE BY MEASURING

Everyone has individual measures they can apply to the job that they control and are responsible for. These are the measures they will be able to improve (see Developing Job Measures, page 99). It's knowing what you are trying to do with a measure that's important — not what you measure. Find out what to measure by measuring.

Start with any measure that seems likely to help what you want to do. Refine it as you learn about the measure and the relative importance of things that have an impact on the job. Change measures appropriately once you have a feel for how the process works. Repeat this cycle as often as necessary to find measures that help. After a few cycles, you will know more about what measures are useful than anyone who only studies the subject of measurement. If kept at persistently, measures that permit the improvement you want will be found. It's an iterative process, best done a little bit at a time all the time.

Using measures properly requires understanding a companion to measures — the principle of variation. Every process has variation, and continual reduction of variation leads to Productive Quality.

A MINI-PRIMER ON VARIATION

The world operates on what is known popularly as the "bell-shaped curve," which is shown in Figure 1. This curve is known in mathematics as the *normal curve* and plots the equation known as the law of errors or the normal law. In many books on statistics and probability the curve is called the *normal distribution curve,* and it's easy to see how "bell curve" evolved from formal mathematics.

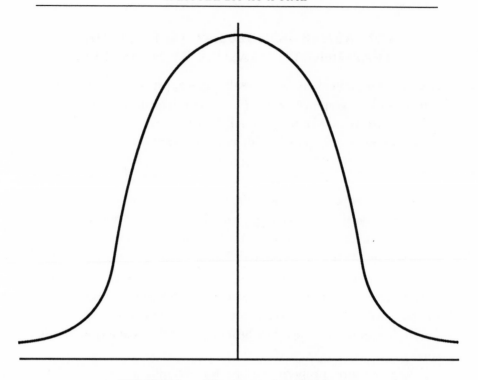

FIGURE 1 — The Normal or Bell Curve

Stop people on the street and weigh them; the distribution will be like Figure 1. The same figure is arrived at if you plot the time it takes to drive to work over the same route, the yield of good wafers going through a diffusion furnace in a semiconductor factory, the age of the workers on an assembly line, or the probability of the location of an electron. It's a measure of how the world works. It's not good or bad — it just is.

The normal curve occurs only if the process being measured is "in control," i.e., the variations in the process are due only to random changes. For example, weigh only people that pass by on the street, not an occasional cat or dog. When measuring results at work, always use the same measuring procedure; it has to be capable of yielding a consistent result for a consistent input. If in control, 98% of the outputs of the process will fall within a specified distance from the center of the curve. You may not like the absolute value of the process outputs — the process may not be capable of giving the desired results. But if it is in control, you will get the same (good or bad) range of results consistently. If the process being measured is not in control, then the output is not predictable and there is no normal curve.

This fact has given rise to a measurement technique known as Statistical Process Control or SPC. In essence, if measures show deviation from the normal curve, nonrandom problems are occurring and corrective action has to be taken. If the normal curve is consistently obtained, then the process is in control and is doing as well as can be expected. In this case, if you do not like the output results, the process, the system, or both has to be changed — exhorting the workers to work harder or smarter or whatever will not, and cannot, help.

SPC is only one of many useful measurement techniques that give a baseline as to how work is progressing. The more important concept to pursue is working continually to reduce variation, even if the process is in control and the final output is "in spec." This is the key to using measures to get Productive Quality.

It is often perceived that if the process is in control and the output is "in spec," then the results are as good as can be expected, that now you should focus your efforts on keeping the process in control. Any further reductions in variation essentially would mean a tighter spec and would not be productive — costs would go up without compensating benefits. But reduced variation does not mean "tighter specs." It means both higher quality *and* higher productivity. Let's go back to Abner Doubleday to see what I mean.

ABNER DOUBLEDAY AGAIN — WITH REDUCED VARIATION

Consider a pitcher whose job is to get the batter out. Since there is no defense against a walk, the first task of the pitcher is to throw strikes. Plotting the results of throwing the ball over the plate in the strike zone produces a distribution like that shown in Figure 1 — the normal curve. We have a process that is in control. If the specification is to get the ball over the plate in the strike zone, then these pitches are quality pitches — they meet the specification.

But pitching to win includes much more than just getting the ball over the plate. A better quality pitch (a Productive Quality pitch) is needed, but no change can be made in the size of the strike zone (the specification). The better quality pitch is obtained by continual improvement of the pitching process to reduce the variation of the normal curve. My favorite example is Warren Spahn, a left-hander who pitched in the major leagues for 21 years and won 363 games despite being out for three years during World War II. Near the end of his career, Spahn said he could throw nearly any pitch — except one down the middle of the plate. He just wanted the outside two inches. The hitter could have the rest. Spahn succeeded by reduced variation.

Figure 2 shows what is meant by reduced variation. The specification hasn't changed. Any pitch in the original strike zone is still a strike. But through continual improvement, Spahn's normal curve had reduced variation greatly and was centered near the outside edge of the plate. The result was that his pitches were more difficult to hit than other pitches meeting specification. This meant there was a higher probability that the batter would make an out when trying to hit such a pitch. This results in a higher probability of winning. Spahn had achieved Productive Quality.

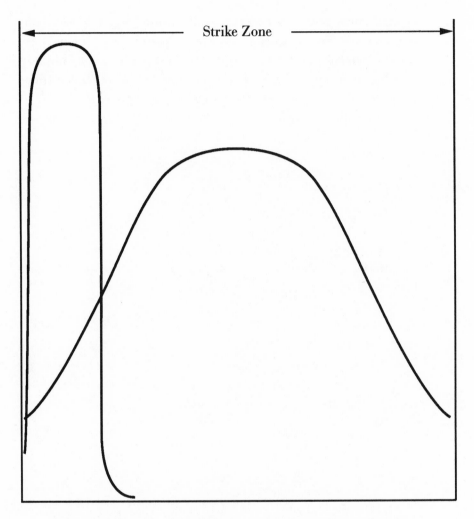

Strike Zone

FIGURE 2 — The Normal Curve and Reduced Variation

Warren Spahn's career ran from the late '40s to the mid '60s. During exactly the same period the Japanese struggled to develop the Total Quality system. They both built on the same foundation — continual improvement through reduced variation. The result for Spahn was a normal curve that covered only the outside corner of the plate. The result for the Japanese was parts that occupied a narrower normal curve within a constant specification range. This meant parts with higher yields and that were easier to use in the next assembly, and end products and that were of superior quality because they had reduced variation — and lower prices. Whether it's Abner Doubleday or everyday, Productive Quality is a winner.

CHAPTER 7

THE END OF THE BEGINNING

A FTER a successful battle following a series of disappointments in the early days of World War II, Winston Churchill said: "This is not the end, or even the beginning of the end, but it is, perhaps, the end of the beginning." I always thought this was an especially apt phrase — Churchill was very good at apt phrases — and I decided to borrow it for use here.

You know what you are trying to do, have a management framework for doing it, and understand the Total Quality and Measures concepts. As Churchill said, you are now at the end of the beginning. You are ready to move out for the main part of the journey — *how* to get Productive Quality..

Continue to focus on what you are trying to do. In summary, the three steps are:

1. Get and keep only the best people.

2. Make clear to them what needs to be done — define the job in terms of good performance and results.

3. Let them do it — create conditions in which they can do what needs to be done.

The management philosophy or framework to operate within when implementing these three steps is:

1. A little bit at a time all the time has the highest probability of success.

2. Leading beats managing.

39

A Total Quality sampler and a Measures primer are included in the beginning because these two subjects apply to the actions you will take to implement the three steps. In summary:

1. Total Quality (TQ) is a proven operating approach based on the three steps and the management philosophy listed above. It stresses individual responsibility for quality and the continual improvement that leads to Productive Quality. It's useful to understand TQ because many of the ways in which we want people to perform are similar to those stressed in TQ. But if the three steps are done consistently, there's no need to install a full-blown TQ system. Any reasonable management approach applied consistently can be made to work if it's based on the three steps. You get the best return on your investment by simply concentrating on doing those three steps.

2. Measures are the key to knowing if the final results you want are obtained, and the key to continual improvement of those results. However, focus on measures that are in the control of individuals and on the continual reduction of variation to get the maximum benefits from using measures.

With this in mind, turn to the chapters that tell *how* to do what you want to do, starting with the most important section, *Section II — Getting and Keeping Only the Best People.*

GETTING AND KEEPING ONLY THE BEST PEOPLE

CHAPTER 8

HOW TO GET AND KEEP ONLY THE BEST

MANY meetings have been called to address "cosmic" issues such as how to do things "smarter," get better productivity, improve the market share, and (in more instances than I personally care to remember) keep from going down the tubes. Nearly always, after reviewing the wish lists, the conclusion has been that the number one priority was getting and/or keeping good people. The need was for more good people, or for specific good people (a new marketing manager or product development team), or *any* good people (clunkers were predominant — excepting, of course, those participating in the meeting).

There is no good company without good people. This seems self-evident, but you need to be reminded of it again and again. It is the first priority. Time spent concentrating on teamwork is wasted if you're not working on getting a great team. Almost everything else can be done wrong in terms of management techniques, organizations, and operating theories and you can still make it if there are good people. The reverse is not true. Most already recognize the importance of getting and keeping good people — what needs to be discussed is *how* to do it.

The *how* is the thing that most miss. Of course you try to get the best people. When hiring or on recruiting trips, you always go after the best. No one is at the schools looking for graduates with grade point averages of 2.0 or less. No one calls up his or her friends and says: "I'm looking for a manager — do you have any clunkers you can recommend? This is an important job so I really need a first-class loser."

No, no one does that. But what they *do* is look for good people *only* when they are in the market for people. That's the problem. That's not good enough. Winners look for good people *all the time* and grab one the minute they find one, whether they "need" them or not. And equally important (yes, *equally* important), they conduct a constant search within the company to find the best and worst performers. Then they work hard to keep the former and move out the latter (one of the best ways to keep the former is to move out the latter). Very few people do *these* things. Those who do accumulate the good performers. Those who do not struggle to get the best they can from what's available at the time they look. Looking only when you have a position open means you have a very low probability of getting good people.

Think in a new way about the process of finding, hiring, reviewing, and transferring people. This is the single most important task for a manager — and it is not a "best effort" task. There are very specific, nearly routine actions you can take that will greatly increase the probability of assembling the best team available for any specific job. Once the team exists, then work on teamwork and all the other things that increase the probability of the team doing well. It takes substantial time and effort to get the best team, but the return on that investment can be better than on any other you make.

THE FRAMEWORK FOR ACTION

You get and keep only the best people by following four concepts:

1. Acquiring and keeping good people is the most important task for managers.

2. Good people are hard to find; search for them continually and acquire them regardless of "openings."

3. Removing poor performers from an organization is as important as finding good ones; the best time to remove them is right now.

4. Changing people and organizations regularly to get the right person in the right job gets the most out of the best performers and helps marginal performers become good performers. It is also much more likely to result in a "contented" and productive work force than is the "stability" of an unchanging organization.

The specific actions that support these concepts are discussed in an overview form below.

THE ACTIONS TO TAKE

Regularly meet and talk with everyone one-to-one. One-to-one meetings help you to identify good and bad performers and to find out what they want to do (or can do). Hold one-to-one meetings in addition to those used for reviewing project status. In one-to-one meetings, focus on learning whether people understand what you are trying to do and whether they can do it. "Regularly" means meeting with one person once a week. (For example, you meet with each of the top 25 people twice a year in one-to-one meetings.) It's necessary to have weekly meetings with key people for such things as project reviews, but one-to-one meetings have a much different purpose, and twice a year is enough to achieve that purpose. If each manager down the management tree does the same, *everyone* in the organization gets reviewed at the same rate.

Always be in a recruiting mode. There are not enough good people to go around, and the probability that one will go by the window just as you are looking out is much too low. Open wide your window of opportunity — always be "hiring." It can be done, head count freezes or no. And it must be done.

Recruit people at the highest possible level. To the customer, the person behind the counter is the company. Get the best person, not the cheapest. The assembler on the line

45

determines the payoff of millions of dollars in design and tooling. Get the best everywhere. You break even when eight "expensive" people paid 25% more do the work of ten "cheap" people. The expensive people are also much more likely to drive continual improvement by throwing in a batch of priceless ideas for free. Go after the best and pay accordingly; less of them are needed than the "cheap" kind.

Reorganize and rotate regularly on a planned basis. Aim for a productive organization — not an attractive organization chart. Reorganization is a good thing if it's part of an intelligent plan to keep improving. It's not something to be avoided and does not reflect failure. Who cares how it used to be done? The idea is to win today. The right person in the right job is the foundation of productivity. Learn the proper fit by trying different people in different jobs. It's a learning experience that everyone should share. It's not just for entry level or new people. Why should they have all the fun — and the opportunity?

Transfer your poorest performers (the lowest 10%) in a permanent flow. The idea is to get and *keep* only the best people. Transfer poor performers with as much diligence as you use in getting the good performers. You will never keep credibility when you talk pay and promotion based on good performance if poor performers remain. You know who the poor ones are, and — more importantly — so do your people. When the lowest 10% is transferred and replaced with people just above the organization's performance median, the center of the normal curve of performance improves constantly and the variation of results shrinks constantly.

The operative word for this action is "transfer." Transfer poor performers to an assignment that fits much better than the one they have been doing. There are always people who don't belong in the company, and they must be "transferred" out of the company. But most poor performers (especially as the level of people is upgraded continually) are just mismatched with what you need done in your organization. Their performance may be poor *in comparison* with others in the same position, but they can be good performers somewhere else in the company. Either way, the job is to make the transfer — wherever the person's destination may be.

Working with the union. The last chapter in this section addresses the hows of working with people who are covered by a union contract. Work as effectively with them as with nonunion personnel. But remember, they have struck a separate agreement that defines parts of the relationship. It's your job (and especially the supervisor's job) to understand that agreement as well as or better than the union counterparts. Therein lies the beginning of wisdom. When the ground rules are understood, all can play in the game. Then the actions outlined above can be applied.

CHAPTER 9

MEETING AND TALKING
WITH EVERYONE
ONE-TO-ONE

A TASK FOR ALL SEASONS

TALKING to people is a tool you should use constantly, and I want to stress its importance up front. It is more than a motivational tool — however good it may be for that purpose. Talking to people is the best tool for gathering the hard data needed to do the actions discussed in this book.

Section III of the book covers how to make clear to workers what needs to be done. That is done best by talking to them. Section IV is about how you make it possible for them to do what needs to be done. Find out what keeps them from doing what needs to be done by talking to them. In this section you will learn how to identify the best and poorest performers, how to transfer those that should be transferred, how to organize and rotate to take advantage of the talents you have, and who to put in the key interface positions. Again, this information is found by talking to people. The key method for these talks is the one-to-one meeting.

WHAT YOU DO IN
ONE-TO-ONE MEETINGS

In a one-to-one meeting, top people in the operation talk about subjects that help each to learn about the other. Do not discuss progress on tasks (that's another meeting) or salary reviews (that's also another meeting). Discuss what your people want to do, what their background and capabilities are, what they need to help them do their jobs, and how they should perform and why. Any other subject that helps both of you learn can be added. Schedule a one-hour one-to-one meeting with a different person each week. This means two one-to-one meetings a year with the top 25 people in the organization (a total of 50 meetings). In those meetings you will learn:

1. Who in the organization is in the top 10% and the lowest 10% in terms of performance and performance *potential.* The top and bottom 10% are the easiest categories to determine (the in-between levels are hard to pin down), and it's in these two categories that key personnel actions take place.

2. Who wants to do what kind of work (and who *can* do what kind of work).

3. The problems that keep people from doing a more effective job. This is hard data that determines how systems need to be changed.

Your people will learn how they are expected to perform and what criteria to use to determine if they've done a good or bad job. They can't do a good job until they understand what a good job is.

If this sounds like too big a return for an hour a week, remember that discussions of this type are rarely held on a consistent, ongoing basis. These kinds of issues usually get discussed — often obliquely — only at review time. At that point, they tend to be outweighed by the emotional issue of how big the pay increase is (or isn't) that year. A specific meeting held for the purpose of learning the above information is much more effective than most people can imagine.

THE ONE-TO-ONE MEETING PROCESS

The one-to-one meeting has no forms, no actions, no follow-ups, no documents of any type. Learning about each other is a process best done a little bit at a time all the time. To ensure it is done all the time, it has to be a simple process. (The probability of continuing a process perceived as being above and beyond your basic job is inversely proportional to the complexity of the process.)

The topics for discussion are those outlined previously. But the intent is to learn about each other, and any subject can help do that — including who won the game over the weekend. In my meetings the rule was to discuss first what was on my people's lists — if *they* wanted to bring lists (the only requirement was to show up and talk). Then I led the discussion on those topics listed above that still needed to be covered.

I took notes in a notebook I used just for these meetings. But there was no intent to make a list of actions to be pursued. I take notes in all meetings, both as a mechanical aid to concentrate on what's being said and as a reminder of what was said — something very easy to forget when it's not written down. It helped that everyone knew I took such notes, and no one was intimidated by the process. This was the only paperwork involved in the meeting and it was for my purposes. Nothing was required of the other person in the meeting.

The goal is to meet at least twice a year with as many people in the organization as possible. If the meetings are restricted to one a week so that an ongoing process can be assured, your limit is the top 25 people. That's more than enough (especially if managers under you extend the process downwards). If you personally know and can rate the organization's top 25 people you can take the necessary actions intelligently to keep only the best people and get them into the right jobs. A sample of 25 is large enough to give you a good idea of what's happening throughout the organization. It also provides a good foundation for others to carry the message downwards.

The one-to-one meeting has no formal sequence that determines the order in which you talk to people. Start at the top of the organization chart and go down, skipping people if their schedules do not match the meeting time that week (go down the chart in horizontal sweeps so that you talk to all the people at the same level rather than just the people in a single group). The people that are missed can reschedule their meetings. If everyone has a list of who is scheduled, they can trade off among themselves and/or reschedule without needing to check with you. Talk with whoever shows up at meeting time. Remember, if the process is simple it can be sustained.

Newly hired people move onto the scheduled meeting list two months after they start so they have some time to become acclimated, but they move to the top of the list so they don't wait through a full cycle. In one year, talk with your 25 people twice (if you have fewer than 25 people, talk to them more often — so much the better). Start over at the beginning each time a cycle is completed. Never stop.

Resist the urge to try to meet with someone more often than once a week. This leads to postponed meetings, which can erode the credibility of the meetings' importance. It also upsets those who must be rescheduled when their peers have already had their meeting with "the boss." If limited to one a week, the one-to-one meeting gets priority like a staff meeting; they happen all the time, and people respond accordingly. Think simple.

KEEPING THE PROCESS "PURE"

One-to-one meetings are not a substitute for staff meetings or regular review meetings of ongoing projects. Those meetings have different goals — and benefits. Continuing them keeps topics that should be covered in those meetings from creeping into the one-to-one meetings. Meeting with individuals on a regular basis to review the status of projects (I always did this weekly) is an important part of management. But this is not a one-to-one meeting as defined here. The one-to-one meeting is quite different and must be kept "pure" — otherwise it will become just another meeting and you will not learn what is needed.

A key part of making this process work is leadership by example. If people follow your example and have one-to-one meetings with their people, then everyone will learn the formal and most valuable subjects to discuss in this type of meeting and will act accordingly. For that reason, the most effective one-to-one meetings are held with people who have one-to-one meetings of their own.

51

LEARNING FROM THE PROCESS

I can't overemphasize the usefulness of the one-to-one meeting. You learn things that can't be learned any other way. People respond positively because they know that whatever else may happen, they are going to get their chance to be heard at least twice a year. If that sounds too infrequent, how many times a year do the top 25 people in your organization get to talk with you now on one-to-one type issues? I'll bet it's less than twice a year — if at all, for most of them. Twice is far better than not at all — and it's enough to learn what you need to know.

In addition to what you learn about people, they learn the intent of encouraging job transfers and organization changes (as the rest of this section will urge). They will see that the best work environment is not a "stable," unchanging organization but one that is changed easily to create constant opportunities. They can be sure what they want to do is clear to you because they will have told you one-to-one.

It seems obvious to simply ask people if you want to find out what they think about something. But think about how rarely this is done for the kinds of topics discussed in one-to-one meetings. There is no need for long discussions and multiple meetings to get a good feel for people and their capabilities. A few one-to-one meetings do that very nicely. People don't need to hear over and over how they are expected to perform and what kind of performance factors are important. Whether they will or can do these things is another issue — but they learn readily what is expected when told one-to-one. The leverage of the one-to-one meeting is very high — that's why two per year will achieve your goals. It's another time investment with a very high payback.

CHAPTER 10

BEING IN A PERMANENT
RECRUITING MODE

RECRUITING IS FOREVER

C OLLEGE coaches speak eloquently about the importance of recruiting. They can be experts on play design, game plans, training, and conditioning, but they know none of this contributes as
much to winning as getting the best players. Coaching can make a
difference between two teams of about equal ability, but no technique will overcome a lack of talent. The only way to assure a supply
of talent is to recruit it.

Coaches know the real name of their game — regardless of the
sport — is recruiting. Many coaches quit because of it. It can be
painful, tiring, even demeaning — and it has to be done on a year-
round basis. All year, every year. Some coaches complain that they
spend only four months a year coaching and eight months recruiting.
Actually, it's more like four and twelve because recruiting goes on
during the playing season. Some assistant coaches never get to see
their team play. On game days they're at other games — taking part
in the recruiting process.

This applies directly to the business organization. Recruiting is
crucial because you can't win without the best players. But to recruit
successfully, it has to be done all year, every year, even if it is sometimes a painful, tiring, and demeaning task. If it was easy to do, everybody would do it well and there would be no winners and losers.
But it's not easy, there are winners and losers, and that creates an opportunity to win. The little bit at a time all the time concept applies
especially well to recruiting.

53

Two key tenets define the framework of recruiting. First, recruit permanently, don't just add people when needed. Second, recruit *within* the company as well as outside. People within the company are prescreened and you get the chance to observe them at work — a chance not available with outside people. Some of the most attractive recruits come to your place of work every morning. Recruit them permanently as well.

KEEPING THE WINDOW OF OPPORTUNITY OPEN

The space program popularized the term "launch windows" — the time brackets for a launch to reach the proper orbit. It's not enough to get everything ready for launch — it has to occur at the time that the window is open — or wait for the next opportunity. In recruiting, the window of opportunity matching the availability of a good person to the time you are looking for people is too narrow to permit an accumulation of good people.

You receive resumes that make you wish you had a spot open for what looks to be an outstanding performer — or that you had that resume last March when desperate for a section head. Calls have come from good people (inside and outside the company) looking for a job just after you've filled a position — and calls have been made to good people who were looking but are no longer available now that you have just the right opening.

That window is small indeed — and it is especially small when you are looking for the best people. Good people go fast and they often move without going on the open market. They are recruited by someone who knows where they are and who checks often to see if they can be tempted to move. Asking on a regular basis increases the probability of asking when they are in the mood to move. That's exactly the role you want to play.

Open your window wide to maximize the probability of getting good people when they are available. Do this by operating on the basis that there are permanent openings and you are looking constantly for people to fill them.

FREEZES AND CUTBACKS
ARE OPPORTUNITY TIME

Most managers have been through enough head count freezes to have frostbite, and most have gone through their share of cutbacks as well. You can be sure there will be more of each in the future. Those are not times to stop recruiting — in fact, they are the best times to recruit.

There's a saying to the effect that "knowing you're going to be hanged in the morning concentrates the mind wonderfully." Similarly, the pressure of a head count freeze or cutback may force what should always be happening — moving out the poorest performers (see Transferring the Lowest 10%, page 70). In most head count actions, all heads count the same — from entry level personnel to all-stars. One can be added as long as one is subtracted simultaneously (or two — sometimes a two for one trade is required). Your willingness to trade maintains recruiting in a period when more good people than usual may be available from managers who are not willing to operate this way. They see cutbacks/freezes as a time when they have to hunker down and give up people.

This is a good time to point out that permanent recruiting does not mean permanent increases in head count. Many people make this mistake and assume permanent recruiting is impossible. Add people slowly as they are found and remove people at the same rate. The head count increases only in a growth mode, but it is not directly tied to recruiting. The probability of *finding* good people is improved by permanent recruiting. Hiring them assumes taking whatever actions are necessary to keep the head count at an appropriate level.

A beneficial side effect of permanent recruiting is never having to crank up a crisis recruiting effort to fill an unexpected opening. This reduces the pressure to hire the first warm body capable of finding its way to the office at the appointed interview hour. When a large field to select from is created, the probability of selecting only the best is increased.

HOW TO RECRUIT
ON A PERMANENT BASIS

The first key tenet is to recruit *permanently.* Do this by adopting the mindset of always looking for people and acting accordingly. Specifically, do a minimum of four things:

1. Let *everyone* know you are looking for people permanently. Tell your people (the one-to-one meetings are ideal vehicles); tell your peers (they'll send resumes of good people they don't think they have "openings" for — you know better); tell the human resources department (always have open requisitions on file and bug them for resumes); and tell outside sources such as colleges you are involved with, friends who work at other companies, professional contacts, etc. Establish a mindset — *always* be looking for people.

Once the pump is primed, keep confirming your interest. One of the questions most asked in professional circles is: "Do you know anyone who's looking for people?" The word travels fast when you become known as one of the "anyones." You will get a steady flow of resumes. Better yet, there will be calls from people interested in making a change who never put their resumes in general circulation (or calls from people who know about such people — either call will do).

Your name should come up in conversations when someone confides to a friend that he or she is "looking" — there are always people who are planning to move because of a personality dispute, a lack of opportunity in their job, or a desire to try something else. The reasons are endless. When the "do you know anyone who's looking . . ." question is asked in the parking lots, cafeterias, tennis courts, and bars of the world, your name should be mentioned. The bad will come along with the good with this kind of method, but you will find good people that you wouldn't otherwise know existed. This is a classic little bit at a time all the time exercise. Keep at it persistently.

2. Keep a *simple* list of people in the company who appear to be in the "good" category. The simplest list is nothing more than a list of names. Follow-up and analysis is neither necessary nor desirable. If the process is too complex it won't be kept up.

Remember you are always recruiting. When you see someone acting well under stress in a meeting and/or their performance strikes a warm chord, get their name and write it down. (I kept my list in the back of the notebook I used for my one-to-one meetings.) Know who the good people are and be ready when opportunity knocks at the recruiting door. Don't pirate people from peers, but recognize the names of people who are looking and are on your list. Know where to offer legitimate promotional opportunities and who you definitely want to keep when organizations merge.

This list is a good source and is painless to assemble. Over the years, literally thousands of people will participate in the many meetings you'll attend, and you will see them perform under stress. Only a small percentage will be recruited, but over several years you will acquire an impressive group — a little bit at a time all the time.

3. Spend an hour each week ensuring that resumes are reviewed and replies are made to inquiries. Be sure that it is done and don't do it alone. Get your people involved in this process with you. Ultimately, they need to agree that the new kid on the block is more desirable than the person being replaced. Reply to resumes and inquiries consistently. It's the only way people will believe you are serious about the process and will continue to forward inputs.

Don't worry that an hour a week won't be enough. Resumes can be skimmed quickly — if it is made a regular task. Doing this on a regular basis teaches you to have a little tingle in your gut when a potentially good one appears. If many people in the organization put in their weekly one hour of review time, a lot of inputs can be screened to find those few good ones. You're looking *just* for the good ones, remember.

4. Interview at least one person a month, every month. This can be someone recommended to you, someone you call in, or someone to meet for lunch. Having interviews less frequently than once a month indicates that not enough attention is being spent on the previous three items. It's a perfect feedback system. Interviewing one person each month keeps your interview skills sharp and gives you a feel for the kind of talent available. Without interviews on a regular basis, you start to lose the capability to recognize a potential 10 when one goes by. As with any other skill, you have to practice the skill of recognizing good people.

This does *not* mean that you or other key people interview everyone hired in the organization, or even a high fraction of them. Your people know who the good ones are as well as you do. It means only that you should have a high enough flow of recruits that you are interviewing at a monthly rate. Performing this function will force good things to continue to happen.

THE RECRUITING FRAME OF MIND

The objective is to create a recruiting frame of mind. Manage as if you always have an opening (and you always do for good people) and proceed with actions to fill that opening — tell everybody you're looking, inside as well as outside the company; consistently process the inputs received; and interview on a regular basis. If this is done all the time, the mistakes often made in the panic mode of hiring will be avoided, and the probability that you will find and hire only the best people will increase greatly.

Now turn your attention to the kind of people to recruit in this permanent recruiting process.

RECRUITING AT THE HIGHEST POSSIBLE LEVEL — AT ALL LEVELS

EXPENSIVE COMPARED TO WHAT?

W HEN the best people are recruited, they are also the most expensive people. But ask the question: "Expensive compared to what?" When the total cost to the company is considered, hiring the best person for the job is most economical, even if they carry the highest salary.

Don't hire someone making $60K for a job typically paid in the low 30s with a $40K maximum salary grade. That's not the right kind of job for someone at a $60K level. The market provides a first-order screening so that people who *want* to do the kind of work defined by a $30K job will be in the approximate salary range. However, do hire someone at $40K if they are clearly the best available for that job. The job's grade level may need to be increased, or you may plan to transfer the person to a job with a higher grade after a year to avoid the grade maximum. But hire the best available person — don't fall back to second best because they'll take $30K a year. Hiring less than the best is the worst kind of false economy.

Eight good people who seize the responsibility and authority given to them will do the work of ten who just follow orders. They will do the job better, defining and expanding its perimeters in ways never thought of before. The result is paying each "expensive" individual 25% more and still getting more value for the money in terms of output per unit cost. People determine the job's worth. A cheap person will make it a cheap job. A high-level person will make it a high-level job. (In Eastern Europe, where pay levels are set universally low, workers have an appropriate saying — "They pretend to pay me, I pretend to work.")

When recruiting, aim high. Get the best; you have a job that is worth the effort of the best person. Give that person the chance to make the job into an even better job. If you set out to get the best person and are willing to pay them what they are worth, you will find who you are looking for.

HIRE THE HIGHEST LEVEL AT ALL LEVELS

Normal business practice encourages you to aim for the best when hiring people for middle and upper management positions. At these levels, salary ranges and job descriptions are extremely flexible to help hire high-level people. However, in jobs below the "management" level there is much less flexibility. The promise of the false economy of hiring less than the best often wins out. Lower level people are hired and have a great negative impact. This includes line supervisors (a very critical spot) and "service" people who interface with other company personnel at service desks, counters, and computer terminals throughout the company. Recruit only the very best here (and everywhere).

Think about service people for a moment. The people who have service jobs determine whether a service system works or fails, and, equally important, they will have the best opportunity to make recommendations for improving the system (see Making Clear Who Is Responsible for What, page 158, about the need to define the responsibilities of service functions). If the cheapest people are hired, the worst possible results occur in terms of service dispensed and credibility of the systems among the users, and system defects that could be fixed will go unrecognized. The costs of services provided ineffectively are much higher than most people think. The ad hoc systems (or "system beaters," see Attaching Authority to Responsibility, page 164, for more on this subject) built to get around the formal systems that don't work — or that don't appear to work — are real killers. The costs of trying to beat poorly implemented systems do not show up on the balance sheet directly against the organizations that hire on the cheap, but that's where they belong — and these unnecessary costs would pay several times over for people who can do the job the way it should be done.

Human resources is an example of an area where this mistake can often be made. The professional managers in human resources understand the critical contribution human resources can make to the company's success (they deal with its most important resource — its people), but human resources policies are implemented almost entirely by people below the "management" level and that's where the bulk of the company's personnel has its communication with human resources — and where the bulk of the complaints occur. There seems to be a perception that the average salary in the human resources area should be lower than most other areas. This is a serious mistake. If anything, the pay should be unusually high to get only the very best people *at all levels*. Typically, not a large number of people work in a human resources department. Hiring only the best (and most expensive) at all levels in the human resources department would have very little impact on the total salary cost of the company. But it would have a dramatic impact on the quality of the implementation of company policy and the perception of the effectiveness of that policy.

But don't pick on the human resources department (however much fun that seems to be) as the only area with this problem: The stores personnel who think the signal to reorder is an empty bin; the clerk in receiving who has no idea where your hot shipment is and no intention of finding it anytime soon and even less intention of letting you take it after you've climbed over the counter and found it yourself. These people represent a failure at the interface point. People and their jobs do not fit each other.

The system fails because the company has gotten people representing the "lowest bid," and these people are not capable of understanding that their job is to deliver a service and that they should do whatever it takes to deliver that service. Making clear what needs to be done (the second step) is not enough. You have to recruit people who have the basic capability to perform *in the manner needed* or the system is not going to work.

Review the interface jobs in your operation. The salary grades for many of them may need to be raised. The old idea of developing a brilliant detailed system to be run by interchangeable bodies is no longer good enough — if it ever was. You need to establish only the framework of a system if it's run by people who know the results that you want. They will use their intelligence and ambition to get those results in more effective ways than could have been dreamed of when the framework was being developed. That's how to improve the system constantly. To improve your operation you need good people, and to get good people you need to pay well.

FOCUS ON THE FIRST LINE

An increasingly important interface point is first line supervision. This is where the people in the trenches must be convinced that management means what they say about commitment to Productive Quality. First line supervision is an important part of the "management team." It is a tough job and should be staffed and paid accordingly. The pay level should reflect the fact that there are more places to get design engineers than there are to get *good* supervisors.

And below the first line supervisor, you still want only the best people. The assembler on the line determines the success of millions of dollars spent in engineering design and tooling. Have the best possible people in that position. If the assembler has a hard time choosing between this job and a routine job elsewhere that is marginally above minimum wage, the line does not have the proper pay classification. Raise it and get the best people everywhere.

To make top management decisions a reality, capable people are needed at all levels of the company to implement what needs to be done. Anyone who hires on the cheap breaks the chain of performance. Good people at "lower levels" can figure out how to get the job done and recommend ways to fix a poorly designed system, but no system design will overcome incapable people. The effectiveness of good people is multiplied many times when they have other good people to interface with at every level in the company.

USE THE EXISTING SALARY STRUCTURE

You don't need to have a salary structure higher than your competitors, or to upgrade all salary levels by X%. What is necessary is the mindset to hire the best person available, not the cheapest person who seems capable of doing the job's minimum requirements. This may put many people into the higher salary grade ranges and the average payroll *rate* may be higher. But if this is the result of hiring only the best, total payroll costs will be lower because you can do more with *fewer* people. Hiring the best always yields an excellent return on investment — at all levels.

CHAPTER 12

REORGANIZING AND ROTATING REGULARLY

A NEW VERSION OF THE THREE R'S

THE THREE R's — reorganize /rotate /regularly — helps get the right person in the right job. It's a cultural change for those who believe organization charts should be changed rarely because people are more comfortable with stable organizations. But the most "comfortable" organization is one where people feel confident they can get a job they like and do well (the two are nearly inseparable). An organization that changes to fit the talents of the people available is the most attractive for good people.

Aim for a productive organization, not a "stable" one (keep stable *values*, not a stable organization chart). *Plan* to reorganize and to rotate (R and R, if you will) on a *regular* basis. The operative words are *plan* and *regular*. Make R and R part of an intelligent plan to keep doing things better, not a response to some unexpected event (good or bad) that forces it to happen. Change is not something to be avoided because it reflects failure or crisis. Who cares how it used to be done? The idea is to win now. The right person in the right job is the foundation of productivity, and R and R is a good way to get them there.

R and R is also a tool for getting good people when they are available. Don't turn down the best regional marketing manager you ever saw because there's only five regional managers on the staff and there are already five good managers. Create a sixth region. Create a national manager for one of the product lines and do everything else regionally. Create a customer manager for your biggest customer. That's creative R and R. Don't miss a good person for the sake of a line of boxes on a piece of paper. Lines are erasable. Good people are hard to get, the best people are rare. The organization of your operation should be part of the solution for *getting* and *keeping* them — not part of the problem.

R and R gives you an opportunity to address problems in different ways and to learn by doing. No one is smart enough to set up an organization that will fit all future changes in personnel and types of problems. If people know that intelligent R and R changes are encouraged, they will recommend ways to make the organization help them — and the people doing the work know better than anyone what changes would help (this is valuable input you get from one-to-one meetings). Individual positions can be created to let someone try something different or to solve a specific problem. After the experiment is done, or the person with a particular talent moves on to something else, eliminate the position. Don't fill it just because it's there. Think of R and R as the creative use of erasers.

HOW DO WE DO IT?

The perception that an organization change is an admission of failure — something didn't work out so there is need to change the organization or to move people into another job — is a major problem to overcome. Understand that the organization is a management tool and use it as such. Sometimes do a little R and R just to keep things fresh and give everyone a chance to look at problems in a different way.

The way to get people to understand this approach is to tell them. Tell them in one-to-one meetings, staff meetings, "all hands" meetings, and when talking in the hallways and elevators. Make it clear that this is how you view organizations and how you plan to use them. Tell everyone what you plan to do and why. Talking to people works every time.

Then *do* what you say. Make R and R changes part of the agenda of regular review meetings. Ask for ideas and get people to think about how to perform better. Work at finding an idea to implement to show that anybody can propose an R and R change — they're not just handed down from on high. Their ideas lead to the changes that really pay off — those the people down in the trenches need to do things better.

ORGANIZATIONS ARE IMPORTANT — GET THEM RIGHT

Regular R and R changes do not mean that organization charts are not important. Quite the contrary. Many organizations have improved dramatically with a small change. Getting the right organization is a big deal. The right group of people with the right chemistry gives everyone the chance to do their best. That's why you should be willing to change so readily. Getting the optimum mix is important and the best way to get it is to keep trying until you find what works for the current circumstances. The mix of people and problems changes constantly; expect the organization to change constantly.

Make the effort to keep organization charts updated and present them in a professional way; it demonstrates that they are important. An old, outdated chart that everybody giggles over ("this is our latest chart but we're really not organized that way now") is a signal that the organization is not considered to be important. It *is* important. Because it's important it's worth thinking about changes that will improve it. And that's the attitude to establish.

THE GOOD WAY TO RUN AROUND IN CIRCLES — ROTATE

Rotate in every way. In a large company, rotate people through different jobs within the organization, in and out of the organization within the company, and through the organization as part of a formal company plan for new hires. The first two approaches often are thought of as transfers, and only the last is thought of as rotation. But don't make such distinctions — all moves can be part of a rotational frame of mind.

People should feel free to move from job to job in the company. If it's looked on as rotation, they can come and go as circumstances change. There's no sense that they are abandoning one organization for another, or should move only if a promotion is involved. There's nothing wrong when someone on a formal rotation says, "Stop the rotation I want to get off." If they think they've found the ideal job, let them stay. Maybe it is the ideal job. If not, they can "rotate" to another one later.

This type of rotation involves money and time — two of the assets in shortest supply in any company (with the exception, perhaps, of enough good people). Make the investment in moving people, training them, and accepting some unproductive start-ups in new jobs. When you land the right person in the right job, the results are outstanding. Freedom of movement is often a key to keeping good people — and also helps to get them in the first place.

Be evenhanded when talking about rotation. Not only encourage people to rotate within your organization, also encourage people to leave the organization to rotate within the company. Tell peers that your people are encouraged to rotate in the company and they can talk to your workers about new positions any time they want. You expect the same courtesy (the list of potential recruits developed in Being in a Permanent Recruiting Mode, page 53, will be very useful here). Everyone has to practice this approach to make it work well.

THE R & R FRAME OF MIND

Keep R and R in perspective. Don't worry that the organization chart will be changing weekly as people sprint through the corridors, rotating from job to job. R and R is a frame of mind. People should know they can change if they want to change. Such change is not only acceptable, it's encouraged. Further, they should give you ideas on how to rotate. That frame of mind is 90% of the benefit of R and R.

When the R and R frame of mind is established, the probability is increased that changes recommended by workers at all levels will lead more of the right people to find the right job. People will be comfortable because they know change is possible. That's what you're after. The number of people who actually move and the number of times the organization chart is changed will be much less than you might think. The difference will be that your people will trigger many of the changes for the right reasons, and you won't have to initiate as many of the changes or make as many in response to people leaving for the wrong reasons. This is the difference that leads to Productive Quality.

R and R also takes a different form. People move at your insistence and the destination is *out* of the organization. It's a very important part of R and R — transferring out the poorest performers.

CHAPTER 13

TRANSFERRING THE
LOWEST 10%

. . . KEEP ONLY THE BEST

YOUR GOAL is to get and keep only the best performers. Transferring performers in the lowest 10% of your organization improves the average performance continually and makes the organization even more attractive to good people. Transferring the poorest performers has a double positive effect.

This is a hard thing for managers to do. They know they should. They know why and usually even know how. But they can't bring themselves to do it. Sometimes they don't like to confront the people involved — even though the best way to help the careers of the poorer performers is to move them to another job. Sometimes they just don't want to start what can become a tedious and painful process of paperwork and meetings and, in the case of large companies, battles with human resources. Often it's a combination of both reasons. But it's easier a little bit at a time *all the time*, and, however hard or easy it is, it has to be done.

Keeping poor performers means they accumulate over time. You want exactly the opposite. Transferring them out of the organization makes room for the high performers who are brought on board constantly. Perhaps most important, transferring poor performers helps you maintain credibility with the 90% of your people not in the outward flow. Few things turn off good performers as strongly as the presence of poor performers whose poor performance is tolerated. They know who the poor performers are — and so do you (the one-to-one meetings make their presence inescapable). It's part of your contract with people to transfer the poor performers.

WHAT YOU ARE TRYING TO DO

Poor performers are the lowest performing 10% of *your* organization. They may be acceptable on an absolute basis, but if 90% of your people are better, then everyone will be much better off if the poorer performers are moved. Since you know 25 people on a one-to-one level, the task is to see that two to three of these people are transferred each year. If each manager does the same, 10% of the entire organization is affected directly. Transferring two to three people each year on a regular basis is a manageable task for each manager.

Note that the operative word is "transfer." Most poor performers are people in the wrong job or the wrong organization — or both. Their poor performance is relative and they can be good performers in another job. The task is to get them transferred to that job. It's a win-win situation, even if it is unpleasant to tell someone that they don't fit into your organization. Poor performers who are not up to the standards of the company need to be transferred out of the company. That's more difficult, but it steadily becomes a smaller and smaller portion of the total work force if you keep adding good people and keep transferring the bottom 10%.

Be sure you've done your part in terms of training and making clear what's expected. If that has been done well, then the best solution for poor performance is a transfer. How you happened to end up together is irrelevant. Most often it's a result of misunderstandings in terms of what they can and want to do and what you want and need done in the job. This usually happens during the recruiting process or when the nature of the job changes. However it happened, poor performers are not going to do well in your organization. There's no point in waiting for the star to come up in the East that will produce the miraculous change — transfer them now.

Some people evolve into a category I call "eye rollers." Most people know at least one. Mention his name and people roll their eyes toward heaven and say "what did he do this time?" He has an extra last name as in "you know how *he* is." Yes, I know how he is — and so do you. He's not a good performer. He might have potential or

71

have been good once, and might even be terrific in the future — but right now he is not a good performer.

There is nothing wrong with people who do outstanding things in unusual and/or outspoken ways. They are often a lot of fun and they don't so much cause eyes to roll as they cause heads to nod in reluctant admiration. They are keepers. But an eye roller does nothing special except keep those eyes rolling. Normal output that requires abnormal amount of relationship patching is poor performance. Alarm bells should go off when you find eye rollers — it's transfer time.

Mathematically stated, you are trying to achieve reduced variation in the performance curve with a constantly increasing median. This is the difference between winners and losers — winners have good people from top to bottom. Their reserve players on the bench could be starting players for most organizations. That's the kind of bench you want. Another look at the normal curve will make clear what you are trying to do.

THE PRINCIPLE OF REDUCED VARIATION — ONE MORE TIME

Figure 3 shows a normal curve for performance. If the lowest 10% is replaced with performers *just above the median,* the variation of the curve is reduced and the median moves to the right (in the direction of higher performance). Thus, the average performance level increases and the difference between individuals' performance shrinks. Overall higher performance can be expected, and you will get nearly equal results from assigning any individual to any equivalent job. The ideal world.

The good news is that to approach this ideal world, you only need to replace the lowest 10% with people just above the median — replacements need to perform in just the top 50%, not the top 10%. This procedure works with mathematical certainty. Figure 3 is a plot of what happens after ten cycles of replacing the lowest 10% of each successive curve with people just past the new median. If you find the results hard to believe, I encourage you to put arbitrary numbers on the initial curve and go through the exercise yourself.

But the lowest 10% must be replaced *all the time* and new people added above the median *all the time.* If not, the distribution moves inexorably towards the left as good people move on or retire. In professional sports, this is the principle behind the practice of giving poorer teams first pick in the draft. The intent is to get teams with nearly identical distributions so that scores are close and game attendance is high. Poorer teams replace poor performers with the best in the draft while the best teams have less to choose from. The best teams are pushed constantly to the left and the worst move constantly to the right.

As the median moves to the right, it gets tougher to upgrade the distribution. However, it gets easier to transfer the lowest 10% because on an absolute basis they are better performers. If I had to select one factor that drives Productive Quality, this is it. This is how to get the people who can do what needs to be done, and who can do it better than the competition. Keep transferring that lowest 10% and keep adding above the median — all the time.

HOW TO TRANSFER THEM

The key is the phrase "all the time" — this is not a one-shot process that is triggered once a year at salary review time or when an eye roller causes eyes to roll once too often. This is an ongoing process that is discussed constantly with the managers under you in review and one-to-one meetings. It's important that the managers agree with you on the 10% pool. They need to be an active part of the transfer process, not innocent bystanders to the mad ax wielder at the top.

Speaking of managers, be sure you review their performance when you review who falls in the bottom 10%. Too often managers who don't perform get moved to "special assignments" or similar ambiguous job descriptions. The perception of the troops is that a manager who doesn't perform is rewarded with a job where he or she

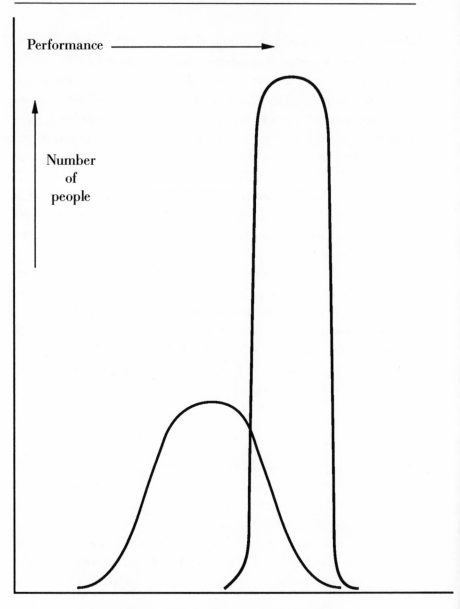

FIGURE 3—Improvement of the Normal Curve
by replacing the Lowest 10%

is not expected to do much while still drawing a high salary. Poorly performing managers are the most important category to transfer. Their potential for doing damage is much higher due to their higher position. Transfer your poor performers and lead by example.

To make the transfer process work, take these four actions:

1. Constantly identify the people to be transferred and make the status of the transfers a priority item. Make specific progress each week.

2. Tell the transferees *now* and tell them honestly why the transfer must be made.

3. For a fixed period of time (nominally two months), give the transferees full time to work on finding another job. That's their new assignment. They know best what they want to do and what trade-offs they can make.

4. In the case of a large firm, tell the human resources department what you are doing and why, but accept that it is *your* job to do the forced transferring. Human resources walks a narrow line here between acting as a service function and acting as the advocate of last resort for all employees. Follow the rules; human resources is the local expert. It's *your* job to work with human resources to develop a transfer plan to which all can agree.

Let's look at each of these four actions in detail.

1. Constantly identify the people to be transferred . . .

The identification process should be part of regular review meetings and one-to-one meetings. Identification is not hard. You know who the poor performers are. The problem is that no planned action is taken on a regular basis to transfer them. The same poor performers show up year after year. You want to fix that.

List the transferees and ask their managers for weekly status. This is as important as any other project they have and they should be as ready to give status on it as on the others (they'll be ready if they know it's going to be reviewed weekly).

Step three describes how to get the transferee to do much of the work, but status reports are necessary for you to know the progress. Remember, it's much easier as a routine process. If done all the time, managers only have to handle two or three transfers a year. If progress is not being made each week, get the transferee and their manager together and find out why.

2. Tell the transferee now and honestly tell them why . . .

Tell the person who needs to be transferred why the action is being taken. Doing this as soon as possible is very important. Do not wait for a "good time." There is no good time. As soon as the person's manager has agreed that it's necessary, do it. Meet with the people who need to transfer, tell them why they do not fit their jobs, and why transfers are required. If you've been honest in past reviews, it shouldn't be a big surprise. But that's academic. When you've decided it must be done, do it — even if it's a "surprise."

There's a strong tendency to give a second or third chance. This is a mistake. If ultimately the person becomes a good performer for someone else, that's wonderful. But when it's not working in your organization and you've done your part of the job, it's time to move them. Don't let it drag on. You can get better performers without nursing a situation that has a low probability of reversing itself. Do it now. Don't be part of the process that lets poor performers hang on.

Be honest about why the move is being made. If you truly view the situation as simply a mismatch and think they are good employees and would fit somewhere else, say so and give some indication of where they might try. Once the flow of people is made an important part of your job, you will learn of openings and the kind of people needed. Tell the employee how to make use of human resources placement programs and tell them that you will help them find a job within the company.

If they are not up to the kind of work done in the company, then tell them. Recommend that they look outside the company, but don't object to their finding a job inside if they can do it. Be honest, however, when telling anyone who asks for a reference why they are being let go. If they can find a job in the company with an honest reference, more power to them. You can't predict what will happen in cases like this. Sometimes an action like this galvanizes people into action. They pull themselves together and sell themselves; their driving force may be to show that you're wrong. Terrific. If that's what it takes to turn them on, it's a good move.

The bottom line of the whole process is to tell them exactly why you want them to transfer and what you are going to tell anyone who asks for a reference. No games in either direction. This is serious business, and it needs to be done right. And it needs to be done now. After you have told them why, be ready for the next step that tells *them* how and that makes the process work.

3. Give the transferees full time to work on finding another job . . .

This is an important step. Give the transferee up to two months full time to find another job. Yes, it really is worth the cost of the two months. The transferees need to understand that their new full-time job is to find a job. They must take the initiative. Give them the time, but they must use it properly (this is the progress that you want in their manager's weekly status reports). Their incentive is better than you might think. If they are basically good employees who are simply misplaced, then they want to find a good job as much as you want them to find it. They will appreciate your being up front and helping them by letting them look full time. But the deadline has to be a real deadline — they have to leave in two months regardless of the status of their job search.

If there is a confrontational situation, the two-month full-time job search assignment is still the best approach. In these cases transferees are not going to be useful employees anyway because the motivation is not right. All of their effort should go into finding new jobs. Constant status reports prevent the problem of them sitting on their hands. This kind of problem happens only occasionally to a given manager, and you simply need to expend more energy on the problem when it does occur. It's the proper place to expend energy.

Be completely honest in this process. Don't go through the "hint" process, and give them nothing but grunt work, hoping they will get the message and look elsewhere, and don't wait for salary review time in hopes that giving them a lousy review and no increase will trigger them to leave. It's not honest and it's not efficient. Instead, put them to work on the task of being transferred. It's a hard task and they can do it best. Tell them you'll help, but the main part of the task is theirs. Tell everyone the transferee is looking for another job. Both of you have mutually decided there's not a fit in the organization. You don't need to expand on that. Everyone understands what's happening. Networking will help locate other opportunities. Then give them the time to do it.

4. In the case of a large firm, tell the human resources department what you are doing and why . . .

Human resources has to walk a narrow line between acting as a service function and acting as the employee's advocate of last resort. In Making Clear Who Is Responsible for What, page 158, I talk in detail about the problems that occur if top management does not clearly define the role of service functions such as human resources, and such a failure of communication can lead to especially difficult confrontations in the transfer process. But even without this problem, the human resources department must practice what they see as appropriate restraint as part of their responsibility to minimize job-related lawsuits. Your job is to make human resources a partner in the transfer process and to learn how to do what needs to be done while operating within the rules (the human resources department is the local expert). Encourage the transferee to talk to human resources and to take advantage of the human resources programs that facilitate internal transfers.

Accept the responsibility to make the transfers happen. This is one of *your* prime tasks — not a human resources task. If top management has done its job, human resources will be a source of guidance and help. If not, human resources will be an obstacle to overcome. In the latter case, work with human resources (and other management as appropriate) to fix the source of the problem, but do not make it an excuse for not taking action.

A FINAL WORD

The final word on the transfer process is do not underestimate its importance. You want only the best people, and failure to transfer poor performers will hurt as much as failure to recruit well. Good performers can be grown internally; show them you are serious about Productive Quality by rewarding only good performance and giving them co-workers who perform equally well. If getting and keeping the best people is made something you work toward all the time, you will find your goal to be achievable and highly rewarding.

CHAPTER 14

WORKING WITH THE UNION

WHAT THE ISSUES ARE

GETTING and keeping only the best people can be applied to union personnel also. There is no need for an "us and them" approach. People's abilities, needs, desires, or responsiveness to intelligent input do not change when they join a union. Cause and effect of disputes do not change either. However, you need to understand some specific concepts to be able to make that application:

1. Union personnel have chosen to work under a contract that defines in advance certain aspects of their relationship with the company. If you do not understand the contract, the relationship will not work. You have to know the rules to play the game.

2. An understanding of the contract is not gained by trying to decide what is "rational" or "sensible" or "fair" or "reasonable." Do not carry this kind of emotional baggage when setting out to learn. The contract is an agreement between two organizations on the conditions under which the group of people it covers will work. It is the result of give and take and compromises on issues whose only relationship is that they are covered in the same document and, therefore, can be paired in the bargaining process. The issue is not "what is fair or sensible," the issue is "what does the contract say?" Understanding this is the beginning of wisdom in union relationships.

3. Like most systems, the contract is implemented by people far away from the point of origin. And like most systems, it succeeds or fails at the point of implementation. The point of im-

plementation in this case is the first line supervisor. If you make no effort to get supervisors who can perform at a high level (remember, you get what you pay for), it shows up strongly in communication with the union. Understanding this is the culmination of wisdom in union relationships.

Now that you have gained the necessary wisdom to know what to do, let's talk about *how* to do it.

WIN OR LOSE WITH SUPERVISION

All of the techniques discussed previously should be pursued with vigor in building a supervisory force. Everything starts with good first line supervision. This is one of the toughest jobs in industry, especially when communication between union and nonunion management is involved. Generally, supervisors are not paid enough and are not rated at a high enough grade level. The first line supervisor should be a key part of your management team. They should be considered one of the most important people and be paid accordingly.

You must make people *want* to be supervisors because of the salary and growth potential associated with the position. Calling the best person in the crew a supervisor and paying them 10% more than the highest level person who reports to them is providing supervision by wishful thinking. The crew may be the right place to find supervisory candidates, but a lot of training and educating needs to be done to make them supervisors. After they go through that sequence, they're worth a lot more than an extra 10%. If good first line supervisors are not acquired, you will have a very difficult time solving the other problems.

THE CONTRACT IS THE BIBLE

Train supervisors to be experts in the union contract. They should be able to pull a copy out of their pockets and address the issues with a higher degree of skill than the union steward. If they can't, they have not been trained properly. Most often the supervisor's copy of the contract (if he or she has one) is in the office and is reasonably clean and in good shape. The steward's copy (usually in pamphlet form) is dirty, tattered, and immediately at hand. That situation has to change. Supervisors should be more knowledgeable than the steward because they are paid more and work harder. Supervisors need and should get lots of training in dealing with people on the line. But the contract *must* come first; it defines the parameters of the job. Once armed with that knowledge, supervisors can put the techniques discussed in this book and all their other training into effect.

Supervisors should not come to you for advice on what they can and cannot do according to the contract. You should go to them. They can come with alternatives and with the probable union reactions to those alternatives so you can decide what to try. But they should be the experts on the contract — not you, and not someone in human resources. Human resources can *help* them understand the contract, but *they* must be the experts on the floor.

In most contracts management has the prerogatives to do things that are not specifically forbidden by the contract. All of the techniques in this book, including rotation and transfers, can be implemented. Their implementation takes longer and requires more discussion and imagination, but can be done. The union will turn the contract on its head to defend jobs, but it will also support changes that give members using higher skills the opportunity to make higher pay, as well as changes that give members the training needed to achieve these higher skills. If supervisors know the contract and are open with the union, they can negotiate the actions required.

Careful selection and retention is just as necessary and beneficial with union workers as with nonunion employees. Line workers know who is and who isn't carrying their share of the load. They know who is making a negative impact on working conditions. They would like to do a good day's work for a good day's pay and to work next to someone who feels the same way. Every good worker wants to do work they can be proud of. But they don't want to feel like fools, working for the same pay as someone who works only half as hard. Support the good performers (the overwhelming majority) by moving out the poorer performers (the lowest 10%).

But if they are union members, move them out in exact accordance with the contract. Keep the records, make the reprimands where appropriate, and take action at the proper time. Don't give it up. Persistence and consistency are absolutely necessary. The union will require absolute adherence to the contract. So should the supervisor. Move people around, reorganize to get the right people in the right job, and transfer people out. The supervisor can do it — if you both recognize that this is a key part of the job and should occupy a substantial part of his or her time.

Support this use of the supervisors' time. Don't expect them to look over the workers' shoulders. Line workers know what needs to be done and how to do it. Supervisors need to find and train and locate the right people in the right jobs, to coach and support the workers, to provide good tools, and to remove the obstacles that keep workers from doing a good job. They are not the local program managers or schedulers or expeditors. Their job is to supervise the workers and develop teams that can do what needs to be done. Your support is the key to the proper use of supervisors' time.

TAKE THE GRIEF OUT OF GRIEVANCES

Another place your support is crucial is in union grievances. There is nothing wrong with a grievance. It is no more important than getting a busy signal on a long distance line. The busy signal tells you that at that time too many people are competing for too few lines. If it happens frequently, then more lines are needed. If it never happens, too much money is being spent on too many lines.

If there is never a grievance, the supervisor is not active enough in trying to get only the best people into the jobs. If you get them continually, someone (not necessarily the supervisor) does not understand the contract or the language needs arbitration. If it does, do it. Arbitration is not a black mark on anyone. Unions are extremely good at pressuring companies that want few grievances and that go to arbitration only when they are sure winners. Unions press the limits of the contract to get benefits for their workers (that's why they exist), and you should be willing to do the same to obtain Productive Quality. Don't be afraid to play the game after you've taken the trouble to understand the rules.

This is not a pitch for confrontational politics. Make sure this message gets across: There must be good lines of communication. The supervisor should never stop telling the steward and the union members exactly what he is doing and why. The workers should tell the supervisor what needs to be changed to improve the process. They know better than anyone and should feed that information back continually. Aim for the best relationship possible between the supervisor and the union.

Within that relationship, supervisors tell everyone that they want only the best and how they propose to have only the best. They are going to do what the contract says, but they intend to have only the best. Then they have to follow through with what's been said and you must back them up. If they do their jobs well, they will get fewer and fewer grievances because the union will recognize they follow the contract and tell workers and stewards in advance what they are trying to do. But the reduction of grievances is not a goal — it is a contingent benefit that comes when supervisors know what they are doing and know how to do it.

GET AND KEEP ONLY
THE BEST . . . ONE MORE TIME

Where do you find this paragon of virtue who is clearly the ideal supervisor? Apply all the techniques of this section to find people who have the capability and then pay them what they are worth. They are worth much more than conventional wisdom says a supervisor should get. Conventional wisdom is wrong. You cannot overestimate the value of a *good* supervisor. Pay them accordingly.

MAKING CLEAR WHAT NEEDS TO BE DONE

CHAPTER 15

THE PROCESS OF MAKING THINGS CLEAR

T HE SECOND step, after getting and keeping only the best people, is
to make clear what needs to be done. To repeat from the introduction: Make clear to them what needs to be done, define the job in
terms of what is considered good performance and what results are
expected.

In this section you will find out how to do each of these things.
First, an overview, and then a separate chapter on each action.

ONCE AGAIN — THERE IS NO SUBSTITUTE FOR COMMUNICATING WITH PEOPLE

Communication involves more than just transmitting a message (see
Practicing the Art of Communication, page 121). The message must
be received, understood, agreed with, and acted upon in creative
ways. This process requires a clear message and an effective means
of transmitting the message.

No means of transmission is more effective than talking with your
people. Don't assume that everyone will get the word eventually. It's
management's job to talk to them directly. You have many forums
for doing so (one-to-one meetings, staff meetings, project review
meetings, all-hands meetings), and they all should be used. By far,
the most effective is the one-to-one meeting. These must occur
throughout the management tree to insure that everyone hears *directly* from "management" exactly what is to be done. That's the
first part of the communication process.

TELL THEM WHAT YOU NEED — NOT JUST WHAT YOU THINK THEY CAN HANDLE

Next, match your discussions to the expected audience. In Section II, you learned how to get and keep only the best people, so plan to work with people who *can* do challenging tasks and who *want* to — people who want to perform. Don't disappoint them after you went to all the trouble to get them. Tell them what really needs doing and what is defined as good performance. Tell them what training you expect them to acquire and what results you expect. Don't worry about overwhelming them. Pay them the compliment of assuming they will be able to figure out how to do what needs to be done. Load them up. Don't try to give them only what you think they can handle. If they can't take the load, then they are the wrong people. Both of you need to find that out as soon as possible.

WHAT IS DEFINED AS GOOD PERFORMANCE

Good performance entails more than a list of specific tasks. The job is not just assembling units, making reports, or responding to directions. Those are only end results. Individuals must perform in a way that helps the whole company get the results it needs. This means addressing jobs in a much broader way than just defining a position's specific tasks. The job is not just to assemble units or make reports or respond to directions. That's only part of the job. The whole job is to satisfy customers, establish good relationships with suppliers, and improve performance continually. When people do the whole job, you have an operation that maximizes the probability of achieving Productive Quality.

No one can guarantee that the function they work in will be a success. Too many things beyond their control can go wrong. But anyone can operate in a way that increases the function's probability of success. If they do that, they are performing well individually. If all indi-

88

viduals perform well, the probability is high that the function will perform well. If all functions perform well, the probability is high that the operation will perform well: It will be an operation with Productive Quality.

That means everyone must do the whole job. Each person should accept responsibility for the quality of what they do, know who their customers and suppliers are, and develop job measures that lead to continual improvement. They should also operate — or perform — or behave — in ways that increase the probability of doing the whole job. Six ground rules define what is considered good performance:

1. Know your individual customers and suppliers. You must know your customers to satisfy them, and know your suppliers to build the good working relationships that mean *consistent* customer satisfaction.

2. Develop job measures that lead to continual improvement in what is done for customers.

3. Know how to set achievable goals and achieve them.

4. Be a constructive complainer.

5. Practice the art of communication.

6. Managers should practice management by walking around (MBWA).

A GOOD PERFORMER UNDERSTANDS THE NEED FOR TRAINING

Good performance includes taking the responsibility to identify your individual training needs and to take the necessary training. And as managers, it's your job to help people find the training they need. The two basic kinds of training to consider are skills training (learning to solder or run a personal computer) and technique training (learning how to listen better and communicate well). Both types are necessary, and the need never ends. Not everybody needs every kind of training, but everybody needs *some* kind of training.

Everybody means everybody — assemblers, supervisors, managers, secretaries, everybody. A large portion of that "everybody" should attend at least one conference or convention each year — that's training also. Your professional group should be exposed to a constant influx of new ideas and ways to improve. The conference doesn't have to be in Hawaii or some other exotic locale — just up the street is fine. Your people will decide what to attend, but be sure they do attend.

Just because what needs to be done is clear to people, don't assume they are equipped to do it — and they can't assume this either. The world changes and everyone needs training to keep up with it. Good people are capable of being trained to do what's needed, and they have the one thing that can't be taught — intelligence.

THE EXPECTED RESULTS

The results you can expect from making things clear include more than just the bottom line numbers. Also focus on the following areas:

1. Good operating methods are a desirable result because you *do* care *how* results are obtained. Heroic efforts to get around systems that don't work are not enough. A big part of doing the whole job is to create systems that *do* work. This is a key result to expect because it leads to *consistent* future results.

2. Make clear the changes that inevitably occur in the priority of desired results. People cannot make intelligent decisions otherwise. Telling people that the desired results are to "maximize profits" or "deliver on time and in budget" is not enough. It's as useless as telling them that all results relative to quality, cost, schedule, and profits are equally important. These criteria have different priorities at different times — that's how the world works. It's your job to be sure people know how the priorities change so that they can adjust the priorities accordingly in their individual jobs.

3. Stress individual results because that's what drives team results. Measure people's performance in their assigned roles. As will be discussed in The Results You Expect, page 139, if no one can run the quarter in less than 60 seconds, the team can't beat four minutes in the mile relay no matter how hard they are urged to do it for the Gipper. Individual results are needed, and you must define them in terms of what is needed *now.* Something always has to be done *now* to meet a final goal — no matter how long term that final goal may be.

4. Get the results by reviewing progress regularly and by asking the right questions. These questions can take the form of a set of measures, but people have to agree that these measures define the role they are trying to play properly. Once agreed on, the proper measures need to be reviewed regularly. As also discussed in The Results You Expect, measuring for the sake of measuring is pointless, and an unreviewed measure will die as surely as an unwatered plant.

Impassioned speeches are often given on the need for "doing better" on Total Quality, productivity, safety, or filling out time cards correctly. The usual response is to implement audits (that measure only end results) and go back to working on schedule and cost because that's where the rewards come from. But the subject of the impassioned speech *can* be improved if it's made part of the expected results and measures are created and *reviewed* to make it happen.

Get your people's agreement on measures that give the individual (and, in turn, the end) results you want, and then review those measures. The actual measures can vary as widely as your imagination can go. The key is to be sure the people being measured agree that the right measures are being used. They must understand the desired results of their individual and team performance and agree the measures being used are the key to obtaining those results.

CHAPTER 16

DOING THE WHOLE JOB

DEFINING THE JOB IN BROAD TERMS

ONE job description fits everyone regardless of their function. That description reads: "Satisfy your customers and develop a good working relationship with your suppliers." Everyone has customers and suppliers. Everyone. Knowing who your customers and suppliers are is the first step in understanding your job. Working with suppliers to satisfy your customers is the essence of your job.

Satisfying customers requires knowing who they are, understanding what they need, and developing job measures that make it possible to provide what they need and improve how it is done continually. When you operate this way, you are doing the *whole* job. That's how everyone should operate.

WHAT IS MEANT BY
DOING THE WHOLE JOB

The line worker executes by assembling part X and part Y. But the whole job is to keep the process in control; to deliver a good assembly to the next worker (the customer), identify problems with the parts he or she receives (from all suppliers including the previous worker), and to improve performance continually by using job measures. Management must create a controllable process (workers' recommendations contribute greatly), but the worker is the key to keeping it in control. Assembling part X and part Y is not the whole job — the worker has to see the job in broader terms.

The clerk in receiving executes by delivering part Z in response to request R. But the whole job is to satisfy the people who request the part (the customers). If the releasing paperwork is mismatched, the clerk works with suppliers (the buyer, the shipper) to satisfy the customer. Producing a properly executed piece of paper saying the part cannot be released is not the whole job.

The quarterback executes by taking the handoff, dropping back five steps, counting to two, and throwing to where the tight end should be. But the whole job is to complete the pass. If the end (his customer) is held up at the line of scrimmage, the quarterback works with his linemen (his suppliers of protection) to create a moving pocket, and throws when and where the tight end comes open. Producing a properly executed pass after two counts that hits the ground (or a defender) is not the whole job. He has to see the job in broad enough terms.

DOING THE WHOLE JOB — WITH TOTAL RESPONSIBILITY

Another aspect of defining the job in broad enough terms is defining the responsibility that goes with the job. This requires that *you* see the job in broad enough terms to transfer the responsibility and authority to the person required to perform it.

For example, in matrix management (see Matrix Management Organizations — Theory and Reality, page 149) someone in each function concentrates on seeing that specific programs progress on schedule and in budget. This person, the functional program manager, reports to the functional manager, but works with the program office (the customer) and functional personnel (the suppliers of both hardware and information) to get the job done. They execute by coordinating and exchanging information on status, problems, and priorities, and focusing on ensuring that the right people have the information needed to perform on the programs and are acting on it.

Assuming the role of functional manager, your job is to concentrate on managing the function, not on the programs passing through the function. Be sure the functional program manager understands that if they do their job perfectly you don't even need to know what programs are going through the function. Their job is not to report results that you can carry forward. You are not the customer. If you are seen as the customer, the nature of what they do and the level at which they do it changes completely. The program office is their customer, and they should deal directly with the customer and the suppliers. The program manager comes to you only when help is needed (your job is to supply that help). Give them the authority to act in this way and avoid becoming a burden by adding meetings they must attend just to exchange information. Carefully defining who their customer is makes it much easier for them to do their job.

Section II discussed the importance of the first line supervisor. That job is not just to supervise the people on the line, though doing the things necessary to get and keep only the best people will occupy a large portion of the time. The supervisor needs to define the customers and suppliers and to work with them accordingly.

Customers require an efficient manufacturing function. They want low cost, good delivery, and the highest quality products coming off the lines — in short, a Productive Quality operation. A first line supervisor has to take the responsibility for training workers to identify customers and suppliers and to develop job measures for continual improvement. The supervisor arranges for the necessary skills and technique training and gets the professional help to do all of these tasks. The job is much more than "supervision," and he or she has to see the job in broad enough terms.

The same concept, doing the whole job, applies to marketing and engineering and plant services and all other functions that make up the operation. All areas have the same job description: See the job in broad enough terms and operate accordingly. They can do so by following the six ground rules (listed in the previous chapter), which are discussed in detail in the next six chapters.

CHAPTER 17

INDIVIDUAL CUSTOMERS
AND SUPPLIERS

A S THE PREVIOUS CHAPTER stated, the "universal job description" is to satisfy customers and develop a good working relationship with suppliers. The focus is knowing *who* your customers and suppliers are.

Identifying customers and suppliers and thinking carefully about your relationships with them helps you see your job in a new way. Recognize that everyone has one or more customers and one or more suppliers. In addition, everyone acts as a customer and supplier to others. When *everyone* thinks in terms of satisfying *their* customer and developing a good working relationship with *their* supplier, the basis for Productive Quality is established.

WHO IS THE CUSTOMER?

Identify your customers by asking what you do and who you do it for. Workers on an assembly line have a customer nearby — the next person or station on the line (*not* the line supervisor). In a matrix management system, a manufacturing function has customers in the program office, engineering, and the downstream manufacturing functions that receive the black boxes they build for installation in the next higher assembly. Their customer is almost never the outside company or consumer who buys the product. A planner's customers are the people who *use* the planning on the floor — not the people who told them to do the planning. The customer of a financial analyst is the person who uses the data to help manage his or her function — not the analyst's supervisor.

95

In short, your customer is almost never the boss or someone out-side the company. You work under the direction and support of the boss; your pay depends on their evaluation of how well the job (which is to satisfy customers) is done, but he or she is not the customer. The outside customer has to be satisfied with the company as a whole or there won't be a company, but that outside customer is rarely *your* customer. Your customers are the people who use *your* output — if they are not satisfied, you have not done your job. The output is not useful. If everyone's customers are satisfied, the output of the company will be useful and the outside customer will be satis-fied.

HOW TO SATISFY THE CUSTOMER

Once the customers are identified, work with them to define their re-quirements in the same way a marketing rep would sell the product or service you work on. If what you supply does not meet *their* re-quirements, then find out why and fix the problem. The concept is to work to satisfy the customers as if they paid your salary.

If *everyone* works on this principle, problems can be solved more quickly because the person who has direct interest in the problem's solution is the person trying to solve it. The change in attitude that occurs minimizes the cry of "it's not my problem." Everyone must take specific responsibility for part of the process.

To keep satisfied customers, extend the marketing analogy. What do customers need beyond what you supply? How can these be met better? What can be done to make it easier for them to do *their* jobs? What do they need that they may not be able to express completely in their requirements to you? If you work constantly to answer these questions, you keep the customer.

WHO ARE THE SUPPLIERS?

Identify suppliers by reversing the customer concept. On the assem-bly line it's the person who sends the item to be worked on. In matrix management, the program office supplies specifications and schedules; engineering supplies drawings and designs and instructions; and the upstream manufacturing department supplies products and parts. The planner and the financial analyst have several suppliers of data, standard forms, and analytical tools. Many more suppliers exist than just outside vendors who are normally associated with the word "supplier."

DEVELOP A GOOD WORKING
RELATIONSHIP WITH SUPPLIERS

How to work with outside suppliers is usually well understood. That doesn't mean it's simple or easy, but what needs to be done is clear. Take the same basic approaches when working with inside suppliers. Make sure your requirements are clear and transmitted intelligently. Talk to suppliers to identify cost drivers, and reduce requirements if those drivers are not essential. As a manager, invite the supplier to meet with customers when they have a problem with the item supplied. Do the same for both inside and outside suppliers (*how* can be different); having a good working relationship with both is crucial to your ability to satisfy customers.

In both cases, be sure to reject or change what doesn't meet your requirements. If standards are set and then bent constantly to accept whatever is sent, you are telling your suppliers (internal or external) that you are not serious about your requirements and that inferior work will be accepted. Inferior supplies are exactly what you will get, and you will not be able to satisfy your customer.

It's clear that developing this kind of relationship with internal suppliers is much easier if they think of their job in terms of satisfying their customers. You're swimming upstream if they see their job only in terms of producing an output rather than satisfying a customer. That's why everyone has to be in the game. Everyone has to operate within the same thought process, and that mode is attained only if it is clear to *everyone* how to operate (it goes without saying that first they have to be capable of operating that way).

THE GOAL IS AN ATTITUDE, NOT A DRILL

It's important to understand that you are after an attitude, a frame of mind in which to operate. You don't want a drill filled with buzz words that die when the next crisis comes, or lists and milestone plans to show how to satisfy customers and develop good working relationships with suppliers. You don't need checklists to categorize everyone as either a customer or supplier.

What is desired under this concept is that people communicate with each other and operate accordingly. Good people only need to know the intent and the rationale of a concept — they'll take care of the details. Supply the intent and rationale, and reward the people who *act* on it. Don't reward those who just make the lists — reward substance, not form. Everyone should ask themselves constantly, "who are my customers, what do I do for them, how can I do it better?" One key to doing it better is to use job measures — the subject of the next chapter.

CHAPTER 18

DEVELOPING JOB MEASURES

HOW TO USE JOB MEASURES

GET organizational results by building on individual results. Get individual results by applying individual job measures. Use job measures to determine if the performance of individual roles is improving and will increase the probablitity of success of acheiving the desired organizational results. As every individual improves continually, so does the organization.

Properly used, job measures help determine if system changes are real improvements rather than just changes. They show where the system needs to be fixed, what alternative to try, and whether the change did any good. They help you understand what your job is and to communicate better about problems by using the data they provide rather than opinions.

Job measures are rarely related directly to the organization's final output because, often, their impact on that output cannot be measured directly. In baseball, the final output is wins, but, because job measures have to be controlled by individuals, only team management can use wins as a direct measure. Individual players use job measures such as home runs, earned run average, and runs produced. As their performance on each measure *improves*, the probability of winning increases.

Sometimes the results of individual roles are hard to measure. When that happens, make *implementation* measures. For example, it's difficult to determine the results of many kinds of "management" training directly. If you are responsible for this kind of training, measure the extent to which you conduct or facilitate training sessions. Implementing training becomes the measure. The key is to define your role in terms of whatever it is that you control, measure how well or often it is done, and improve that measure continually.

Having sanctioned the use of indirect measures when necessary, remember that what is desired, ultimately, are organizational results. Job measures are a vehicle for getting those final results, but have no meaning independent of them. If you are not getting the results you wanted as an organization and/or those results are not improving as job measures are implemented, you have the wrong job measures. Job measures simply give you an individual lever that can be used to improve your contribution to the output of the organization. It may be one measure or many small measures, but the result of improving job measures has to be improvement of organizational results.

HOW TO DEVELOP JOB MEASURES

Develop useful job measures by examining the customer/supplier process. What is done for the customer — what measure would help you do it better? What defects occur regularly in the supplied material — what measure would help remove them? What is the biggest problem in satisfying the customer — what measure would help eliminate that problem? Within this review of the process, obtain the most useful job measures by using the following guidelines:

1. Think small. Job measures should help what you want to do, not be the lead act in a dog and pony show for "management." There is no such thing as a job measure that is too small. Start with the simplest measure that you think will do some good — and don't try to measure *all* aspects of the job at once. Pick any area that needs improving and measure the simplest thing that will help improve it.

2. Do not keep a measure beyond its time. If the problem the measure was meant to solve has been solved — or replaced by a bigger problem — then move on to other measures. Keep them only if they are intended to monitor performance on a contin-

ual basis. Job measures can always change — only the need to measure remains constant.

3. Not everyone needs a different measure. One measure can be useful for many people. If they do similar things and have similar problems, similar measures make sense. The key is for everyone to have at least one measure — not necessarily a different measure.

4. In many jobs there is not an "ideal" measure — no one thing or action to be performed in preference to all others. Try a series of measures and learn by doing. You may discover an optimum measure or continue to use many. Either approach is good as long as there are measures.

5. Everyone controls at least two aspects in the process they work with: (1) their recommendations of how to improve the process, and (2) how effectively they apply themselves to the areas they control. Focusing on these will yield job measures that increase the probability of improvement in the process output, regardless of how indirectly the measures may be tied to output.

DETERMINING WHO SHOULD CHOOSE — AND USE — JOB MEASURES

A job measure is useful only when it's chosen by the person who's going to use it. It will not lead to continual improvement unless the person using it believes he or she can do something to change performance output (they have some control) and believes the measure will help *them* do the job. A measure that looks good on a chart, that management is interested in, or falls into a similar category is not a job measure. It may be useful for some other purpose to some other person but won't do what a job measure is meant to do unless the person using it *chooses* the measure. They can have assistance developing alternatives, but they must find one that fits their definition of "control" and "help" or it won't work.

101

Who can best use job measures? Everyone. The probability of improving any task is directly proportional to a person's ability to create a measure that defines the task. Useful measures for any job can be found with these guidelines. *Any* measure the measurer believes in will do to start. Then try different measures to see which works best. Rarely will one key measure be found because there isn't *one* key measure — there are only measure*s*. Don't try to measure every aspect of the job at once — one problem at a time will do (a little bit at a time . . .), and use simple measures. Counting how frequently something happens is often a fully adequate measure for improving it. Have a *measures mentality* — to improve something, no matter how big or small, find a measure and then improve the outcome of that measure. If everyone thinks this way consistently, all will find *useful* job measures.

A JOB MEASURES SAMPLER

Let's look at specific job measures, based on what has been discussed so far.

An Operator on the Line — A wide range of measures can be developed in this area — items made per unit of time, yields, number of defects, etc. These can be good measures, but be sure to consider the aspect of individual control and process control properly. If the process is not in control, get it in control before attempting to measure or improve the effectiveness of the operator's role. Sometimes the same action will help control *and* improve it, but focus on control first. Then work with the operator to select job measures that will lead to improvements in the process.

Measures such as overall line yield are *not* good job measures for individual operators because they cannot control what happens on the line before or after their station. It's good to tell the operators what yield is needed to make the process viable, and pay incentives if the line exceeds that level — an excellent way of getting everyone to think seriously about ways they can help improve the overall yield. But do not use line yield as a job measure for the individual operator.

102

(It might be a useful job measure for the general manager who has the command of resources to do something about the overall yield.)

Station yield is a good job measure *if* the process is capable of that yield and is in control. But if both of these criteria are met, keeping the process in control and *pursuing ways to improve it* are more beneficial than tracking yield only. Maintaining control of the process and *making recommendations to improve it* are the best job measures for the tasks performed by line operators.

Recommendations for improvement are important. The source of most changes in a process should be the operators of the process. Everyone is in control of recommending improvements. Part of the whole job is to make recommendations. Don't tie each recommendation to a specific degree of improvement at the bottom line; you don't need a complex collection and award system. If you want to make an incremental reward for recommendations, that's fine, but don't let the system for doing so get in the way. Continual improvement is part of the job, not an over-and-above task.

The Training Personnel — Job measures vary with the kinds of training they conduct. If a clear "before" and "after" result directly proportional to the training exists, the difference can be used as a job measure for the people responsible for training. However, many kinds of training don't have payoffs that can be measured directly — you would need a control group of untrained people to see if they do better or worse as problems arise and are dealt with. But it is desirable to train people in multiple disciplines so they have as many resources to call on as possible. If the training is successful, the result is a bottom line that improves continually, even if the incremental gain due to the training isn't shown clearly.

When before and after results can't be identified, focus on making sure the training happens by using job measures that measure the degree of implementation of the training. The managers responsible for having people trained can measure the number of people, the percentage, the subject matter, and when individuals took the training. Measuring who, when, and how many insures that it happens —

103

and managers are in control of these measures. If they keep increasing the percentage of people trained in various disciplines towards 100%, they are continually improving.

The person responsible for conducting the training can make similar measures: How many trained, courses offered versus the demand, and the perceived effectiveness of the training by the trainees (surveys of *their* perceptions are fine). All these measures are in the control of the trainer. Constantly improving them constantly increases the level of training and the probability of improved organizational results.

Implementation measures are excellent job measures in areas like training, where the problem is rarely the quality of training. The problem that occurs is not enough training in terms of quantity and diversity. Job measures that collect data on the degree to which training is implemented help to pinpoint and attack the problem. The information they provide is more valuable than complex attempts to measure the incremental results of training at the bottom line.

The Field Salesperson — Field salespeople are measured universally by sales in their region, and a good portion of their salaries are paid on that basis. There's no question that sales are the desired result; it's a measure that the saleperson should know intimately in terms of what they are and why. But again, the question of control needs to be addressed.

Giving the salesperson a big bonus when a sensational new product sells like gangbusters in their specific region is fair — if they are willing to trade that for a bad year when they do everything right and sales bomb for reasons out of their control. A person whose genes are suited to a boom and bust environment can invent ways to hold those sales up (and their salary with them) that no one would think of in a normal environment. With salespeople of this type, sales will probably be the one and only job measure.

But the fact is that sales are not a measure totally within the salesperson's control. They depend also on the nature of the region, customer base, logistics in the geographical area, changes in the economy, and changes from the previous year in competitive position in terms of price and performance and new preferences in technology — to name just a few variables.

The salesperson is only one factor that contributes to the number of sales in their region. What do they control individually? Many things — all of which can be counted: calls made, people contacted, suggestions made for new products or product improvements, field reports submitted, reports made about competitors' inroads and successes and failures in the area, times contacted by customer service because an order was impossible to read or in error, plant visits and seminars scheduled in their area, trips made to the factory to learn about new products — the list of things they control is a very long one.

Adding up these measures does not give sales, but improving their performance increases the probability of maximizing sales in the region. Thinking about their effect on his or her ability to increase sales tells the salesperson where to concentrate efforts when variables he or she doesn't control turn negative. Job measures also provide lessons to pass on to other salespeople. These job measures can be used in addition to sales to give a sense of control. Essentially, they measure implementation of the act of selling, and, doing so, they increase the probability of getting increased sales.

The Middle Manager — It's perceived that this area is difficult to measure. Middle managers, unlike a salesperson or an assembler, often do not have a primary task. Also they rarely have total control of an operation with distinct results that can be used as a job measure. They are, as the name suggests, in the middle. However, they *can* define a good set of job measures by addressing the management techniques discussed earlier. Once again, measure the implementation of those techniques.

Job measures of this type within a middle manager's control include: number of one-to-one meetings held, time spent doing management by walking around, time spent recruiting, time spent transferring the bottom 10% (and a list of why they are and when

105

they are to be transferred), number and percentage of the people who know their customers and suppliers and who have at least one job measure (remember, the manager can also use only one job measure at a time — everything doesn't have to be measured all the time).

If managers are doing these things well (using measures help them learn *how* to do them well), then they are doing a good job of measuring; it's fine to pay bonuses based on bottom line results. It's a good way to keep managers with the company and thinking about their contributions to the bottom line. But measure them on what they control if you want to measure *their* performance. When everyone performs well, the company performs well.

"Let me tell you my problem" and *"One of these days we should" Measures* — These two are the most common introductory phrases when someone comes up with a job measure. Listen carefully to hear the measure needed. "My big problem is that receiving takes too long getting stuff from dock to stores." Or, "one of these days we should see how long it takes to get stuff off the dock." That's just what to do — create a measure to find out. The process of measuring will uncover the biggest delay, and that's the first step to improvement.

The list of problems that can be improved with job measures that begin with these phrases is endless. The in-house machine shop is "too expensive" — by how much and compared to what? Too many people are out sick on Mondays and it kills our efficiency — how many people is "too many" and how many dollars are "killed"? The drawings are full of errors and it costs a fortune to make changes — how many errors correspond to "full of" and how much is that "fortune"? One of these days we should find out what our turnover is, one of these days we should find out how much all this overtime costs, one of these days we should find out how many hours we lose because equipment is down. Yes, you should.

Convert "we should" into "we did" by measuring. Once the baseline is known, action can be taken to improve it. Doing this over and over is how to get continual improvement. If the problem can't be described with data, you don't know what you're talking about. You can't communicate well to someone who can help fix the problem. Complaining regularly about people being out sick results in the boss getting sick of hearing about it. Complaining that the line is always short 9% on Mondays will generally get attention, and complaining that the line is 9% short on Mondays and costs $X a month as a result will *always* get attention. Now you're speaking a language that everyone understands.

THE BOTTOM LINE

The bottom line for job measures is brief — encourage a *measures mentality* to identify measures for every job. Then improve those measures continually — as a result, improve the company continually. This idea ties into the next chapter, which covers setting and achieving goals.

CHAPTER 19

SETTING ACHIEVABLE GOALS AND ACHIEVING THEM

GOALS ARE A USEFUL TOOL IF . . .

USING goals as a management tool is a subject of some controversy. The flavor of the argument against their use is that the concept is flawed because factors beyond the control of the individual have a greater effect on results than the performance of the individual. The same argument has been made against "management by objectives" and similar concepts.

Those who support the process of setting and working towards achieving goals say it leads people to operate in ways that substantially increase the probability of success. However, this is true only if the goals — like job measures — can be achieved individually. Otherwise there is no cause and effect. A good test of whether a goal is achievable by an individual is whether a job measure can be set. If not, it isn't a useful goal.

A GOALS PRIMER

Set useful goals using the following guidelines:

1. An individual goal should be achievable by the individual who sets it.

2. Set the number of goals carefully. Too many is far worse than too few.

3. Think small — goals are achieved by working in small increments persistently (a little bit at a time all the time). The

longer the time required to achieve a goal, the greater the need to break the goal into small increments, so achieving a long-term goal is the result of achieving a series of smaller goals. No goal is too small, but many goals are too large.

The first two guidelines help you select goals and the last helps achieve those that have been selected. The major problem with most goals is that they can't be achieved by the person who sets them. The second most common problem is that the goals are too ambitious — don't set out to solve problems in one gulp that have been around for a long time. Knowing how to set goals is a key to learning how to achieve them.

SETTING INDIVIDUALLY ACHIEVABLE GOALS

Because the concept behind them is the same, the rationale used to develop job measures applies directly to goals. Reduce a large overall goal to increments that are the responsibility of an individual and then help them choose individual goals. This results in achievable individual goals, and if individuals meet their goals, the larger goal will be met.

For example, the field salesperson in the job measures example cannot individually achieve a goal of increasing sales in their area by 5%. Too many things beyond their control determine sales. But by breaking down the job into the tasks that lead to increased sales and setting goals to improve the performance of those tasks (making more calls, sending in more field reports, arranging more factory visits, etc.), the salesperson arrives at individually achievable goals that *their* performance can be measured against.

Team goals are discussed a lot today, but team goals are achieved by individuals accomplishing individual goals. The best example is Abner Doubleday. Only management can work toward a goal of increased wins for the team. Players can be paid incentives based on wins to ensure wins are their priority, if choices have to be made between individual and team performance. But each individual must meet goals tied to measures, like runs batted in and earned run average, for the team to have any hope of meeting its goal of more wins.

The problem of individual goals versus team goals is not a simple one. Don't establish competition between individuals in a way that detracts from the final team goal. Two players, trying to outhit each other, can drive up wins but also can cause losses if they focus on individual hits at the expense of team wins. In some cases a player's value is shown by team rather than individual results. When K. C. Jones first began to play regularly for the Boston Celtics, his coach noticed that although Jones' individual statistics were not impressive, the team always seemed to be further ahead when Jones came off the court than when Jones had gone in. His conclusion was that Jones should play as much as possible.

Try to avoid assigning goals beyond the control of the person responsible for the goal. An individual player can rarely be measured fairly by team results (Jones and others like him are exceptions). So use individually achievable goals but make sure everyone understands the team goal and does not concentrate on their own goal at the expense of the team goal. Setting goals to make specific profit margins or to deliver on a complex program on a specific date or to increase productivity by X% are goals that usually apply to a few high-level people. Over 90% of your people must have individual goals that they control or you will be wasting your time with goals.

TOO MANY IS FAR WORSE THAN TOO FEW

How many is an important part of setting credible and useful goals. One goal that's met is better than a number of goals that can't be met. The minimum number of goals per year is one. The maximum number can also be one. Meeting one useful goal a year for ten years puts you far ahead of people who list ten big goals each year and never reach them. The idea is to set goals and meet them. People who set too many are not thinking about what they are doing. Anyone can set a lot of goals. It takes intelligent management to set and achieve what can actually be done.

There's an argument that says if too few goals are made, everyone will achieve those that are set without being challenged. Frankly, it would be nice to have the "problem" of everyone achieving their goals. That's not the issue. The issue is that every time a meeting is held to list organizational problems the same list reappears (and a lack of enough good people is right at the top). These problems are never solved through crash efforts, which end in frustration. Next year the same list is made again because the problems require complex actions far beyond the control of any single person or team.

Accept the fact that the problems were developed over several years and it will take several years to solve them. If one "big" problem a year is solved, five will be solved in the next five years. That's a lot better than what's happened in the past five years. A little bit at a time all the time works as well with goals as it does with everything else.

THINK SMALL

The third guideline is to think small — focus on working persistently in small increments. For example, when a goal is set to do a sizeable study, it is often difficult to get started because it is assumed a big block of time is needed — and big blocks of time are hard to come by.

The solution to the problem is not to try to figure out how to create big blocks of time; the study can be done using small blocks of time. Setting aside fifteen minutes in the morning and fifteen minutes in the afternoon to work on the study is an achievable goal. In one month, ten hours of work can be given to the project. Doing it in small pieces lets the iterative process work between sessions. It creates time for information to be dug up while the analysis is still being developed. Doing something right *now*, no matter how small, always pays extra benefits.

If your goal is to make 500 sales calls this year, don't think of it as 500 calls a year. It's ten calls a week which is two calls a day which is one call every morning and one call every afternoon. That's an achievable goal — one that can be worked at right now. Every goal can be broken into small chunks in one way or another, and breaking them into such chunks is the way to make desired results happen.

"SMALL GOALS" — WITH BIG POTENTIAL

Using goals to achieve "small" objectives can have high potential payoffs. Most often goals are thought of in terms of "big" issues — profits, programs, and production schedules. But the process of setting and achieving goals can also be used to take actions that increase the probability that people will be more productive, though performance on the job cannot be tied directly to meeting those goals. These goals are related to career development and address the issues there is never "enough time" to pursue.

Examples of career development goals are reading books and taking courses in your field, having internal "management" courses, and meeting regularly with people with whom you work. These goals should continue indefinitely and they need to be pursued in a way that makes them achievable on an ongoing basis. Often they are pursued on a crash basis, leading to frustration and finally the abandonment of the goal. There's a better way — think small and about what *can* be achieved.

Broaden your knowledge by reading in your field, but don't set a goal to read a book every week to make up for books not read in the past. Try assigning 15 minutes twice a week to reading. Even a slow reader will do 6,000 words a week. That's a book of 60,000 words (about the size of this one) in ten weeks. That's five books a year — or 25 books in five years — in 30 minutes a week.

The same can be done with courses in your field. Start with one course a year. A course can be started and dropped and another substituted and still the goal of one per year can be met. Going to class isn't oppressive. But setting a goal that requires going to class every week of the year begs for failure.

Courses that teach management techniques and how to handle and communicate with people are worth taking inside the company on an annual basis. This is an important part of your job and there is always something new worth learning. It's hard to know how good the available courses are before taking them, but the probability of finding the best ones is increased by talking to others who have been through either the course itself or similar courses with the same company or instructor. That's the best place to start. The most important thing is to select one every year. The argument will be that neither you nor your people have the time — but if you think small and chunk, this can be an achievable goal.

The selected course should have a maximum time of two days. Don't complicate the process with follow-up actions and milestones, etc. The course should be useful, not oppressive. Everyone can find two days in a year to attend — as long as attendance is all that's required. Sure it's useful to read material in advance, have discussions, and follow-up actions. But 80% of the value is going, hearing the presentation, and thinking about it as it applies to the operation. That's enough. Doing the rest only adds another 20% of value and usually causes 80% of the gripes about how much time it consumes. Think small. Keep it simple.

Finally, meeting with your peers in other operations can solve small problems before they become big problems, can help you learn better ways to do things, and can make it easier for people in the operations to interact. Having such meetings regularly is a useful goal.

But successful as some of these meetings are, their occurrence may tend to fade over time. They become burdened with too many players and the excessive weight of detailed agendas and actions. What works better are smaller meetings between interested peers who use achievable goals to schedule and conduct meetings.

An achievable goal is a monthly two-person meeting with no agendas, actions, follow-up, or minutes. An achievable goal is to meet with four people individually three times a year (or with each of the four every four months) and talk about common problems and interests. The appropriate job measure for these meetings is a list of the four people and a record of when the meetings were held. Every manager in your organization can select four people with whom they have important interface roles.

When good people meet in this fashion, they find mutual problems and solutions (or the names of people who have solutions) that they can exchange. This process, done over a long period of time, creates bonds in the organization you can't get any other way. It's an easy goal to set, an easy goal to meet, and it works if it's kept simple. No agenda, no actions, just talk. If actions result that both want to pursue, fine. But don't weigh the meeting down or it will be postponed often, then forgotten; marked on the calendar, but never held. Time can be found for such a meeting once a month if it's relatively painless. Make it an achievable goal.

THINKING SMALL

"Small" goals have been discussed to stress the point that what is wanted are goals that can be achieved — not goals that look good in a book of management objectives. If you think about goals in this way, you will learn to set and *achieve* them. Learn how to do that, and you will be able to achieve "big" goals — by persistently achieving a series of small goals.

CHAPTER 20

BE A CONSTRUCTIVE COMPLAINER

THE USE OF CONSTRUCTIVE COMPLAINING

CONSTRUCTIVE complaining is a valuable tool. You want complaints about the things that *stop* people from getting the job done effectively — the stoppers that reduce productivity. But constructive complaining includes the responsibility of recommending how to remove the stoppers. Complaining and then walking away is not constructive complaining. That's griping or — even worse — whining (gripers and whiners are at the bottom of the pit). It's important to make the difference clear to people.

Many people are reluctant to complain. They feel it has the flavor of not being a good soldier and are uncomfortable making a complaint even when they know it is legitimate. Stress to them that complaints are your best feedback on whether or not a system is working, and that complaints from the hardest working and most conscientious people have the greatest impact. Complaints with recommended solutions lead to new ways of doing things that you would often have no other way of knowing.

THE BEST INDICATOR OF A BAD SYSTEM IS WHEN GOOD PEOPLE CAN'T PERFORM

I once led a group responsible for preparing data for a management meeting held every Thursday morning. Our role was to consolidate data and highlight status and trends. At least one inconsistency in each meeting hurt the credibility of the rest of the data. Various solutions were discussed, but when one of my best people said *his* problem was that the input data was consistently late, I focused on that issue.

It turned out to be a common sequence. The data was due from another plant on Monday and often didn't show up until Tuesday. *Routinely,* there simply wasn't enough time to do analysis, compilation, and distribution by a Wednesday afternoon deadline so the line managers could review their data before the meeting. The complaint was not universal because everyone was used to being asked to work on short notice. I knew the prime purpose of the review was trend analysis, and thus the currency of the data was not a big deal. We changed the system to use data from the prior week so we could do a good job of analysis. The problem went away.

It took a complaint from one of my best people to identify the system problem. His complaint was the litmus test. If he couldn't perform, it couldn't be done. What was not needed was a lot of analysis or pep talks about renewed effort. The system needed to be changed.

Encourage complaints from your good people. They test the system every day. They know whether it works or not. An analysis by a great system designer who says it should work is irrelevant. If your best people can't make it work, it doesn't work. This is the most reliable poll. One-to-one meetings uncover constructive complaints as part of the discussion process, but they are given more consistently when people recognize constructive complaining as part of their jobs.

GRIPES VERSUS CONSTRUCTIVE COMPLAINTS

Look for constructive complaints — not gripes (gripes are one of the most readily available commodities in the world — there is never a shortage). The stoppers you want people to identify are those that they don't control and can't change through actions of their own (they are expected to fix the ones they control). Have them tell you the problem and what they think should be done about it, but ask them to keep working on the problem.

Doing what's required as well as possible while saying there's a better way *and working to find it* separates a constructive complaint from a gripe. A constructive complainer keeps performing, and doesn't just hang in there without recommending persistently how to fix the problem. Encourage all the inputs you can get. The best people are those who perform well but also raise issues that would help them perform better.

You never want to hear "I could have told you that would never work" — it's their job to tell you. It's their job to try to make it work (you never know if you don't try), but it's their job to tell you they think there's a better way. If they don't know the details of that better way yet, they can at least find the stopper. Knowing the stopper is a big step towards the solution. But finding the stopper among a batch of gripes is tough. It's much easier to pinpoint with constructive complaints.

THE OFFHAND KILLER

Stoppers are often thought of as "big" problems that grind things to a halt. But that's not really the prime problem of systems. The big stoppers are easy to identify and lots of resources can be brought to bear to get them fixed. The real productivity killers are the 1,000 little things that never get fixed. It's the cumulative effect of these problems that make it hard for you to compete with companies who concentrate on fixing those "little" things. Just like "small" goals, it's the small stoppers you have to seek out and destroy.

An example of this kind of stopper is what I call the "offhand killer." This is a request that often happens in meetings several levels up in a corporation. During a presentation someone says in an offhand manner "it would be interesting to see what that data looks like over the past five years, broken out by region and product line." They might forget they mentioned it by the time the meeting has ended, but it's going to produce lots of feverish effort in the bowels of the organization — usually at the expense of something that really needs to be done ("I know you're busy, but they asked for it up on the tenth floor").

This is as much a stopper as any systemic problem. Consider the return on investment of "staff work" in the same way you consider the return on any other investment. Look at how much effort is required to do what's been requested and whether sales by product by month is really of greater significance than sales by product by quarter because there's already a report that breaks it out by quarter. Or consider that sales by product is a horrendous effort to complete within the time frame requested but sales by product group is no problem at all.

Studies triggered by offhand killers go on for months, even after a few weeks of effort show that the study won't accomplish the intended result. In hundreds of companies around the world, data is collected that is simply filed into notebooks. It's not reviewed and often it's difficult to remember the offhand killer ("you know, we should take a look at . . .") that started the collection process. Procedures resulting from "let's be sure that never happens again" go on long after the need for them has passed. This happens because no one complains — they just comply. Yet the cost of preventing a rare problem often exceeds the total cost resulting if the problem actually happened again. No one reviews the *reasons* for such procedures.

A lot of effort has gone into offhand killers that get a thirty-second review from managers who murmur how interesting the data is, while trying desperately to remember why they asked for it and what in the world they had in mind when they did. One of the problems is the amount of time it took to get the data — the information is no longer topical. Doing the research sooner in a simpler fashion would have made it much more useful.

This does not mean that the managers who ask for such data are a bunch of stiffs. Quite the contrary. They're smart, intelligent, and clever, and they see implications that most people don't even think about. Hence their requests for information not acquired routinely. They know several kinds of data will reflect the trend or indication they suspect is occurring, but someone close to the data needs to tell them what choices are feasible. With this input they know whether the game is worth the candle.

Urge your people to look for these choices and for the easiest way to do the job. Being good soldiers doesn't include swimming across the river in full uniform and pack because that's what they were told to do by a leader who didn't know about the bridge farther downriver. It's the 1,000 small issues like this that people close to the work can fix if they understand the job includes constructive complaining.

CONSTRUCTIVE COMPLAINING AND PERSISTENCE

A Management Philosophy (see page 14) discussed the persistent probability principle. Over time, if something is kept at persistently, the probability of success increases constantly. Constructive complaining works on the same principle. Your people should be "persisters" — as before, the old cliché that "he who persists, wins" is absolutely true.

If all else fails, persisters win by sheer brute force. Sometimes they win because as choices between alternatives get harder to make, the person who sounds a clear and consistent call gets heard. Sometimes they win because their plan stays alive and well while other plans die off as supporters finally give up or get diverted to other issues. Sometimes they win by implementing the plan on their own and presenting a successful result as a *fait accompli*. However it's done, the result is the same — persisters win.

The attitude for your people to have is to persist in efforts to change what doesn't work. They work on the problem, they complain about stoppers, and they persist in their efforts to improve the system. Persistent constructive complaining becomes successful constructive complaining.

TO COMPLAIN WELL, ONE MUST COMMUNICATE WELL

Enough said. Communication is the subject of the next chapter.

CHAPTER 21

PRACTICING THE ART OF COMMUNICATION

IT DOESN'T COME NATURALLY

COMMUNICATION is not just a motherhood issue. If everyone communicates well, the probability of effective information exchange in the operation is increased. That increases the probability that everyone will do *now* what needs to be done *now* (there are no rewards for doing the wrong thing well). Communicating orally and in writing are different skills and neither comes naturally. Everyone hired knows how to speak and how to write, but not all know how to communicate well. It's an acquired skill that one learns primarily by doing. Have your people practice until they learn to do it well — and, then, have them do it regularly.

COMMUNICATION — TRANSMITTER, RECEIVER, AND TRANSMISSION MEDIUM

A communication system has three parts: transmitter, receiver, and transmission medium. There's also a built-in test for determining if the system is working well: If it's not, two phrases — "nobody listens to me" and "nobody tells me anything" — are often heard. Keep this kind of static out of your organization.

Transmission comes first. Make clear what needs to be done; the more you practice, the better you transmit. But no matter how poorly you transmit, poor transmission is infinitely superior to none. Never assume people have the information you want them to have. Tell them regularly and clearly. People who complain "nobody listens to me" need to be sure the proper complaint isn't "no one reads my mind" or "no one hears what I *really* mean to say." The communication channels are crowded — a clear and steady transmission is needed if you want to be heard.

Reception is next. Receiving well is harder to learn than transmitting well. The complaint that "no one tells me anything" often, in reality, is "no one tells me anything enough times" or "no one tells me what I want to hear" ("no" is a transmission that many people choose not to receive). Listening to what is being said rather than waiting for a pause so you can deliver your next burst of transmission is a skill that demands lots of practice. Nothing can be communicated without a functioning receiver.

Third is the *transmission medium*. You can have good transmitters and receivers and still not have good communication because the proper link between them is not made. That link can be oral, written, or visual. There is no "right" choice. The formal and informal organizational structures and systems often define the best choice. Guard against the tendency to use one medium all the time — especially if you are comfortable with only one. Be able to use any medium.

Be willing to vary any of the three parts to fix communication problems. You may want to change frequency or the medium rather than just increasing signal levels if your transmission is not heard well. If some receivers are turned off, try carrier pigeons — or get a friend to turn up their receiver so all can hear. The key is to use whatever combination works.

HOW DO YOU LEARN TO COMMUNICATE WELL?

The short answer is practice. There's a story — told in several versions — of a famous author arriving at a writers' seminar in a state of inebriation that left him ambulatory but far enough advanced to cause him to speak from the heart. Looking at the anxious would-be writers in the auditorium, he asked how many of them *really* wanted to write. When every hand went up he asked, "Then why the hell aren't you home writing?" and wobbled off the stage. End of presentation.

His point has been reiterated by many writers. We learn to write by writing. We learn to communicate by communicating — by practicing writing and speaking and listening. Don't react to opportunities, make a plan to create them. The most common methods of business communication today are presentations, memos, and meetings. Encourage people to practice communicating in all three ways.

THE ART OF COMMUNICATING
THROUGH EFFECTIVE PRESENTATIONS

Start by taking company presentation courses (use leadership by example — if you can find time to do it, so can everyone else). The best courses tape your presentations, which are then critiqued by the instructor and you. The results can be dramatic. After watching your hands going in and out of pockets as if they had a life of their own, hearing the loud jingle of coins and keys, wincing at "you know" and "and, ah," and seeing your back turned towards the audience constantly, a first-time tapee is amenable to help.

These "mechanical problems" can be overcome with simple repetitive practice and a transmitter that transmits clearly can be built. A slow, quiet, low-volume speaker can't be turned into a dynamic, fast, high-volume speaker. You can't redo a squeaky voice, remove a nasal whine, or magically create that absolute sense of confidence some speakers always have (although knowing what you are talking about pardons a lot of sins). But enough improvement can be made to move any intelligent person to the level of transmission where people will listen.

BRING ONLY TEN POUNDS
FOR A TEN-POUND BAG

Don't show up to give an hour-long presentation with a pile of view graphs that can't even be flashed on the screen in an hour, let alone discussed in any meaningful way. In a presentation where discussion is intended, use the rule of thumb of five minutes a view graph. That means an hour presentation needs only 12. Three minutes a view graph is reasonable if the presentation is essentially tutorial. If you try to present more, useful communication is not going to take place at the rate you will have to go.

Presenting too much material insults the audience. It suggests it wasn't worth your effort to make the material fit the allotted time. Often, the excuse is that there were too many questions. But what is the presentation for? If it's a lecture or speech with no planned discussion, then making it fit into the available time is only a question of practice. But if discussion is intended, allow time for it — lots of time. There's no penalty for ending early because there was less discussion than anticipated.

The excuse of too much discussion reminds me of the building contractors who argued against late penalty clauses being invoked in Detroit. They used the excuse of unexpected bad winter weather. Detroit has had bad weather for years; it's hard to accept that it was a surprise to the contractors. Audiences at presentations that are intended to have discussion will ask questions and will expect answers. It's hard to accept that this is a surprise to speakers.

Good communication requires a transmitter and receiver to operate at the same time. When the presentation drones on past the appointed time, receivers click off or walk out with their owners. Learning how to express key issues in few view graphs has the same benefits as learning to get them on one-page memos (see effective writing). Awards are given for good communication, not length of presentation.

The final step in the process of learning how to give presentations is to seek opportunities to present. In many organizations "designated" presenters make most of the presentations — especially if the audience includes higher levels in the organization chart. Encourage the people who do the work to make the presentations. Spread the opportunity to speak around. Get everyone involved — one learns by doing and whoever is not making presentations is not learning to communicate in a way that is important in every company.

LEARNING THE ART OF COMMUNICATING THROUGH EFFECTIVE WRITING

The value of written media is underestimated. It is thought of as slow and old fashioned in a world of computer-based telephones, where much of the conversation involves planning to "get together" to solve a problem. But used properly, written notes save time and money and speed up the decision-making process. The exchange of a few notes can initiate decisions and action in less time than arranging a meeting or scoring a point in the telephone ping-pong game.

You may have asked for the status on a problem and gotten the response that nothing's happened yet because "we keep missing each other on the phone" or "I keep trying to catch him but he's always tied up." I've made many speeches about this problem, linking its occurrence to the many people who have the attitude that the pencil and paper and instructions in their use are obsolete (and who have ignored the invention of the personal computer and word processing software — the advanced model of paper and pencil).

Write a note. It doesn't have to be great literature. "The alternatives are X and Y, please choose and advise." "The question is Z — is the answer yes or no?" This is good use of communication media. Information is exchanged and decisions are made with a minimal expenditure of time and energy. Save the face-to-face or phone-to-phone sessions for issues that really need them. Many reasonably complex issues can be resolved by writing a reply in the margin of a memo or by drafting a memo for the boss to sign. And it can be done in a day — not next week when an open slot can be found to discuss the issue.

A problem can be understood much better if it is confined to a one-page memo. If the key issues can't fit on one page, the essence of the problem isn't understood and is not yet ready to be communicated effectively by any media. Writing a one-page memo is a skill well worth learning, and it's learned by dogged practice.

USING WORD PROCESSORS

Encourage everyone to learn to use a word processor. They lead to better written communication because they facilitate rewriting (which facilitates the iterative process). The best books (and the best memos) are not written — they're *rewritten*. Handwritten memos are composed at a maximum rate of about 30 words a minute, even if abbreviations, which only a secretary understands, are used. The most elementary hunt-and-peek process matches that speed, and the revision phase puts the keyboard further ahead. Those who dictate get long and repetitive sentences because it's hard to organize and edit in your head. The thoughts are there and forcing a flow of words is not a bad way to bring them out. But unless writing is trimmed and condensed afterwards, the message gets buried in a speech. Only the message is desired.

Editing — composing, trimming, condensing — is much easier with a word processor. There's an argument that "typing" is not the best use of your time. But the objective is good communication, and using a word processor produces a surprisingly fast rate of improvement in written communication as the iterative process grows. What you end up with is usually different (and better) than what you wanted to say originally. It *can* be done by editing multiple drafts from a secretary, but the loss of "creative heat" in that method makes it a poorer use of time than inputting the memo yourself.

An approach that incorporates these concepts has worked well for some companies. They require that a one-page memo (the shorter the better), summarizing the issues and stating what is to be decided, be distributed before meetings. These meetings are more effective because the reason for the meeting is clear and participants can go right to the important issues. There are also fewer meetings as people get better and better at expressing in written form (on their word processors) exactly what they are trying to accomplish. Often the necessary decision can be reached through memos.

LEARNING THE ART
OF COMMUNICATING
THROUGH TWO-PERSON MEETINGS

Encouraging people to meet with their peers in two-person meetings is an excellent way to exchange information. It is the essence of good communication — an iterative process that transfers information and stimulates new ideas at the same time.

As discussed in Setting Achievable Goals and Achieving Them (see page 108), such meetings happen by requiring people to meet individually with four other people at the rate of one meeting a month (i.e., three times a year with each of the four persons). The selected four are in other organizations with similar jobs or problems.

Reporting the results of these meetings is not required, nor is having an agenda or developing follow-up actions (none of the trappings that usually kill efforts to continue holding such meetings on a regular basis). The only requirement is to meet and talk.

As expected, these meetings produce a useful exchange of information. But they are also a good tool for learning communication skills. People learn how to initiate discussions that are of mutual interest, how to select useful information to transmit, and how to listen. The more you do it the more you learn — and the better you communicate. And it is a method of communicating that has immediate contingent benefits.

127

COMMUNICATION IN TRANSIT

Although usually not thought of in terms of communication, management by walking around (MBWA) is a form of communication that has many contingent benefits in addition to communicating with a wide range of people. You will learn how to do it in the next chapter.

CHAPTER 22

MANAGING BY WALKING AROUND (MBWA)

MBWA AS AN EXTENDED ONE-TO-ONE MEETING — GATHERING DATA AND COMMUNICATING

HEWLETT-PACKARD (HP) is credited with originating the term "management by walking around." It's not easy to pin down the origin of industry "buzz words," but HP was certainly one of the first and continues to be a strong practitioner of MBWA. The "W" has been used by various proponents as "wandering" or "walking," but I prefer "walking" because it has the flavor of a planned activity. MBWA is best done "informally," but planning makes it effective.

MBWA is exactly what it says. Walking around the operation helps you get the knowledge that is needed to manage and is an excellent vehicle for effective communication. It is like extending the one-to-one meetings outwards. You learn things that you could learn in no other way, and you transmit a message is to your people that you want to learn about problems where the work is being done. All managers should practice the technique, and in all directions (not just downwards in the organization). If it's done widely, the probability of effective managerial decisions increases because the knowledge of how the organization works and how improvements can be made increases substantially.

HOW TO MBWA

The places to "walk" can extend from the area just outside your office to facilities on the other side of the country. The point is to *physically* get out and talk to people where *they* work — and to listen to what is being said. Showing the flag is *not* what you're after. If possible, have an assembler or technician show you around. The supervisor or foreman can tag along, but you gain the most when the workers explain what they are doing and why. While walking, there's lots to do.

Look at the housekeeping and the travelers that go with the tote boxes going through the line. Read the signs on the wall and on the coffee machine and in the rest rooms. Handle the merchandise and sniff the air. Ask people how they could do things better, ask them what stops them from doing their jobs. Listen to the answers.

Don't expect to remember everyone by their first name, but do learn what kinds of skills and personalities and attitudes exist in which areas, what the reactions are to the working conditions and the pronouncements from "on high" (read the comments scrawled on the posted notices), and whether the engineering information and instructions that go out to the floor have the utility they are supposed to have in the real world. For "listening," eyes can often be as effective as ears.

Besides receiving, do some transmitting. Tell workers why the building hasn't been painted for five years. Tell them the company's problems. Tell them when you don't understand why some things are as they are and agree to find out. Give them a sense of what the world is like from *your* perspective. Tell them what you expect from them and why.

The procedure for MBWA is the same whether the walk is through a factory, engineering labs, the accounting department, a computer room, or offices just down the hall. Ask, listen, respond. Doing it consistently over a long period of time will teach you many important things about how the organization works — and doesn't work.

CONSISTENCY AND FOLLOW-UP

MBWA should be a regular routine. There is no prescribed amount. Do as much as the payback justifies. But be willing to think small — an hour a week is fine if done every week (a little bit at a time all the time). Beginning even smaller can make it easy to get started. When people learn you come around on a regular basis, the benefits accumulate sharply. They begin to gather information for your next trip, and they know it's worthwhile to do some things a little out of the ordinary because you'll be back to make note of it. It's worthwhile for them to say what's really going on because something will be done about it — or you'll come back to take the heat if something isn't done. You don't have to go through at the same time every day or week or month — just return on a regular basis.

Be sure to share what you learn. When MBWA is done at levels below yours, you're going to hear from workers what lower level managers won't hear. That's how the world works. Keep workers' information coming by making something happen in response to their input. But you don't want to become a complaint center — local supervisors and managers are the main contact for solving problems — so it's important to pass on the information you receive. If appropriate, you can keep the source anonymous, but without the information no one else can do anything about problems.

Don't clutter the feedback with problem lists, corrective action milestones, and all the other trappings that make efforts like MBWA too complicated and cause their demise. Managers at all levels have to be good enough to solve problems once they know what they are. If problems persist, you'll hear about it the next time MBWA is done in that area — the people will keep track.

FINDING THE TIME TO DO MBWA

At an industry seminar, a manager presented a procedure for tracking costs and stressed the amount of time he had put into the technique to make it work. Afterwards, talking with a manager from HP,

131

the speaker remarked that he had heard of MBWA, thought it was a sound idea, but was so busy tracking costs that he didn't have time for MBWA. The HP manager replied that he thought the presentation was excellent, and he sure wished he could put that much time into it, but he was too busy with MBWA.

There is time to do what you want to do. At HP it is taken for granted that MBWA is a management priority and it is done as a routine part of the job. Other items had to compete for the remaining time. With that approach, everyone "had time" to do MBWA. If kept simple, you will have time to do it too. Just do some amount — however small — on a regular basis. The accumulative results are dramatic.

· PRACTICING MBWA IN ALL DIRECTIONS

MBWA is not restricted to the areas you are responsible for. The same benefits can be had from sideways and upward MBWA as from downward MBWA (the standard direction). MBWA through interface areas helps you understand the impact of your actions on your customers and also helps you understand suppliers' problems. It generates a lot of additional data.

None of this happens by osmosis. When I transferred to a new operation, my first step was to get copies of the facility plan and the organization chart. I checked off names and buildings as I visited them over the next few weeks. I didn't stop until I saw everyone in their areas. It was immensely helpful in getting a feel for the operation, how it was managed, who the key players were, and where I could find what kind of information.

After three months at Hughes, I was giving directions to people who had been there 20 years but weren't sure how to find certain buildings. At meetings, I introduced people who both worked in the same building for ten years. When the division manager started a series of meetings to be held in the offices of the line managers, I gave the assistant division manager directions to the office of a line manager just below his level. That assistant manager had been at Hughes

132

over 30 years and had known the line manager for at least half of that time. He cared about the company, worked hard at making it succeed, and was open to input from anyone at any level. But because they did not have a direct reporting relationship, he had never visited the line manager's office.

These are not unique experiences. They happen everywhere regularly. They represent a loss of potential information sharing and better understanding of how the business can be improved. An hour a week doing MBWA in all directions can make all the difference.

WHO BENEFITS FROM MBWA?

Many people look at MBWA as another "touchy feely" effort that is supposed to help morale. It may or may not, depending on how it is done. Infrequent visits with a retinue, resembling a state event, won't help anyone's morale — and, in fact, can have the opposite effect by appearing to be condescending. Frequent informal visits with questions and answers intelligently asked and given help morale. But boosting morale is only a contingent benefit.

You reap the real benefit from MBWA. You get data needed for managing that cannot be gained in any other way. You add to your storehouse of information about who to keep and who is in the bottom 10%. The iterative process to do things better is triggered, and you make clear to people what is expected of them. Like one-to-one meetings, MBWA is a method for collecting hard data that helps you to manage as well as a vehicle for effective communication. It gives an excellent return on the time you invest.

CHAPTER 23

TRAINING — THE UNIVERSAL NEED

TRAINING IS FOREVER

GOOD people maintain their competitive edge when you help them find the training they need. They are interested in learning, and they apply what they learn. Not everyone needs the same amount and kinds of training, but *everyone* needs *some* training *every* year. Systematic exposure to new skills and new ideas increases the probability of continual improvement. Everyone should take the responsibility for getting the training they need, but as a manager it's *your* job to help them find that training.

DEFINE TRAINING IN BROAD ENOUGH TERMS

Think broadly about training — it's more than sitting in classrooms. In addition to skills and technique training, *plan* training that often occurs only on an ad hoc basis — attending (internal and external) meetings, seminars, and conferences. There's much to be learned from the discussions and presentations as well as from talking to other attendees at lunch, at breaks, at cocktail receptions, and in hotel lobbies. As many people as possible should be exposed to this kind of training. Also think about who could profit from joining you when important meetings (with no attendance restrictions) are held. This is learning by attending, and you should lead by example. Managers should practice the same kind of "on-site" training down the management tree.

As part of this process, plan to have everyone go to an external conference or seminar at least once a year. Everyone means *every*one

— the costs can be quite reasonable, and it's a good investment. Low cost "how to be better" seminars for everyone from secretaries to supervisors take place all over the country. Everyone learns something from such courses, and you benefit from what they learn. If you tell everyone you want them to go, they'll find the right gathering to attend. They know best what they need to know more about. Make such training part of *their* job.

ENCOURAGE BOTH SKILLS
AND TECHNIQUE TRAINING

Skills training includes learning how to solder, run a machine, operate a personal computer, and do a regression analysis. The list is literally endless, but essentially the skills can be learned in a mechanical way.

Technique training includes learning how to manage better, make better use of time, handle people, and how to lead. Many people consider these "touchy feely" courses and they are often viewed with skepticism. However, the ones that work help people and contain at least one new idea. Managers should take at least one such course each year. Let's consider this kind of training first.

TECHNIQUE TRAINING

There are always new techniques to study that will make you think in new ways about doing things — often leading to better ways of doing them. Taking such courses *with* your people increases their value by helping you learn each other's reactions to specific management issues. It doesn't have to be a course that runs into the dozens of hours over several days. Many courses do require that type of time investment and, unfortunately, many managers don't get involved because of it. The investment may be worthwhile, but there's no way to tell that up front. As discussed in Setting Achievable Goals and Achieving Them (see page 108), an achievable goal is to take at least one course (lasting two days, maximum) each year. Doing that *every*

135

year builds a substantial base of knowledge about management techniques. Taking more is fine, but it's the *planned minimum* effort every year that pays off.

Many courses can fit the two-day maximum by eliminating the paperwork that surrounds them — and bogs them down. Again, 80% of the course's value is in the material presented, the discussion about it, and everyone's thoughts about how it applies to their organization and their individual job. The 20% of the value that comes from paperwork (to be read beforehand and/or filled out as "homework" and/or as "participatory" learning) is what produces 80% of the eye rolling and the moaning and groaning that greets announcements of such courses.

Forget about the trappings. Have people attend, talk, think, and leave. That's it. A two-day meeting is a two-day meeting — no preparation, no stretched-out follow-up. When people know that the time investment is rigorously limited, they're willing to make future investments of their time. That's how to make the process work on a regular basis.

An optional approach, which can be very effective, is for the organization's top managers to take the course with their boss and then repeat it with their top people (their one-to-one lists). This results in everyone at a "managerial" level taking the course with his or her boss. It doubles the time investment for those managers between the topmost boss and the first level supervisors, but it can produce a triple play. You learn the subject matter presented and also how the boss and your key people react to it. Doing this consistently makes it much easier for people to learn what you want to do and how you plan to do it.

You can select from many courses. Learn by doing. You will be exposed to clunkers as well as to ideas that you don't know how you got along without. Experimenting is the best way to increase the probability of finding ideas that apply to you and your specific situation.

SKILLS TRAINING

Everyone agrees on the need for skills training, but three things have to be done to insure good results: (1) train people to do the exact task they want to learn, (2) send supervisors through the same training their people take, and (3) train people about the process their task is part of.

TRAINING PEOPLE TO DO
EXACTLY THE TASK TO BE DONE

Train people for the exact task they will perform and preferably on the equipment on which they will actually work. In the NASA soldering class, this means teaching more than how to solder. Teach people how to solder in that tiny little box with connectors in the way and with wire of such small diameter that the engineer ("but we have to get the weight and size down") who specified it is cursed. That's how to get good solder connections in the real world where real work is done.

Training someone on the machine he or she is going to use is tough when there's only one in the place, it runs 24 hours a day and still loses schedule, and the capital budget can't afford another one for the next decade. Still, aim for such training as the baseline and keep trying to figure out how to do it. There's always a way if it's a priority.

MAKING SUPERVISORS
PART OF THE TRAINING

Supervisors have to take the same in-house training their people take. All of it. Otherwise you run the danger of getting the following exchange between supervisors and their people:

"Who told you to do it that way?"

"That's how we did it in the training class."

"Well that's not the way we do it here."

If this scenario occurs, the training has wasted a lot of time and money and you can lose credibility with your people. The stage has also been set for a crisis several weeks from now when the government source inspector rejects a part because the acceptance criteria used is based on what is taught in the training class.

Having supervisors go through the same class as their people not only prevents this problem, the class benefits from their experience, which can be used to help develop the training. Supervisors have a lot at stake; they need well-trained people who know the specific tasks that have to be done. Adding supervisors to the training class insures that it teaches what it is supposed to.

TRAINING ABOUT PROCESSES
AS WELL AS TASKS

When people are trained to develop a skill, whether it be soldering, running a computer terminal, or filling out a form, often they aren't taught that their task is part of a total process. Many potential benefits are missed as a result. First, the basic skill is mastered sooner if the person understands the role they play rather than just knowing the lever they pull. Second, if they understand what the system does, they can recognize when it is not running properly and tell you how to improve it. Third, they can modify their role to make the system work as intended if changes occur that their training did not anticipate.

This approach follows directly from the concept of thinking broadly about training. In training, when information is included about the entire process, people have the tools to tell how to make improvements in the system, not just in their specific part of it. That brings the full return on your training investment, and helps get results — which is the next topic.

CHAPTER 24

THE RESULTS
YOU EXPECT

TELL THEM MORE THAN
JUST THE NUMBERS

TELLING people the expected results involves more than defining key numbers — even though those numbers are very important. If the numbers aren't right, there is no business. But in addition to defining the numbers: include good operating methods as an expected result; make clear the changes that occur in priority among desired results as conditions change; stress individual results as the driver for team results; and review progress regularly by asking the right questions.

HOW YOU GET THE RESULTS
IS IMPORTANT IF YOU WANT
CONSISTENT RESULTS

"I don't care how you do it as long as you do it" is *not* what you want in your operation. Don't accept ongoing heroic efforts to get around systems that don't work. That makes it impossible to get good results *consistently* and, instead, you get unpredictable results — sometimes good, sometimes bad. This is not the way to run your business. Managers should lead the effort to find systems that *do* work. Then results will be consistent — and will provide a baseline for continual improvement.

Make effective development and improvement of systems an expected result. Assign it as an action, review progress, and work on it yourself when required system changes exceed your people's pay grade. (One of *your* most important jobs is to improve systems —

even if it's not a fun job.) You need systems that work. *How* you get results *now* has a lot to do with the results that can be expected to get in the future.

An important caveat helps solve the dilemma between fixing systems or going around them to get the job done. You want good results consistently in forward years but also need results *now* or there may not be any forward years to worry about. So the caveat is to do *now* what needs to be done *now*. But don't let it go at that. If you have to get around the system to perform, the system doesn't work. The system will have to be gotten around permanently. You can't afford that. You will lose to competitors who don't have to expend this kind of energy. Today, it may be easier to take the money and run, but a business can't be built on that basis. Fixing systems that don't work has to be an expected result. It's hard, grimy work, but it has to be done.

EVERYONE MUST UNDERSTAND CHANGES IN EXPECTED RESULTS AS CONDITIONS CHANGE

Output results are defined by some combination of quality, cost, and schedule. This is true whether running a high-volume production line or a high-technology program that produces one item over several years. Working backwards from these desired results, define the interim results for different parts of the organization. Some results are "more equal" than others under certain conditions, and focus has to shift accordingly. The probability of achieving interim and final results increases substantially if people understand the rationale used to develop each set of incremental results.

The basic results desired in an operation are increasing profits and returns. But some years the focus must be on establishing systems and learning to make a profit — any profit. Other years, compound increases in profits and returns can be pursued. People need to understand the context in which immediate results are achieved. "Maximum profits" or "deliver on time and in budget" are not specific enough. Expected results need to be defined more intelligently than that because intelligent people need appropriate information with which to work.

People adjust best to changing priorities in desired results when they know the reasons. Telling them all results are equally important is as useless as telling them nothing at all — maybe even worse. Quality, cost, and schedule are important to you and the customer; profits and returns are uniquely important to you. But different concerns take precedence at different times, and everyone should know it. The why and how of results are as important as the absolute numbers. It's your job to be sure people understand the why and the how. Otherwise their only recourse is to set their own priorities based on their understanding of existing conditions.

YOU LIVE OR DIE ON INDIVIDUAL RESULTS ACHIEVED IN THE PRESENT TIME FRAME

Result goals are stated in terms of program or operation outputs, just as result goals for a sports team are stated in terms of wins — a team output. But remember that a team is only a concept. Individuals performing individual roles produce a team output. It takes a living, breathing individual to hit a home run in the bottom of the ninth — the "team" can't do it. The motivation for that home run should be a desire for the team to win, but send up someone whose individual results say there's a reasonable probability he can hit it out. Measure performance in assigned roles to be sure to get the team results you want. If no one runs the quarter in less than 60 seconds, the team can't beat four minutes in the mile relay no matter how much teamwork is stressed and how hard they are urged to do it for the Gipper.

Further, review *now* the results you want *now.* No matter how far into the future the payoff is, things have to be done now to ensure the payoff comes. Don't play the boo-yea game (boo for now, yea for later). Without immediate results now, there won't be long-term results in the long term. Poor results (on an absolute basis) can be accepted for now if that's what the long-term payoff requires, but go after improvement of those short-term results like you would any other results — starting at the individual level. Ultimately, you will get the desired final results.

GET RESULTS BY REGULARLY
ASKING THE RIGHT QUESTIONS

An old cliché says that the questions are more important than the answers. It fits the flavor of what I call "leadership by asking the right questions." No matter what results are important, people will focus on the questions they are asked. If someone is asked every day how they're doing on cost, cost is what they are going to work on. They're going to be able to answer *that* question. If the decision is to push schedule at the expense of cost but you can't resist asking about costs persistently, the worker will think emphasis is still on costs. If you ask questions about a whole range of "interesting" things beyond those few results that are really important, you give out mixed signals and get mixed results. Ask the right questions to get the right results.

One place to ask questions is in the regular progress reviews that typically use a fixed set of measures. Be sure that these measures represent the right questions. If it's measured and reviewed, it has to be one of the expected results. People should be able to focus on a measure with the confidence that it represents the right thing to do now. If your measures do not fit this scenario, they are the wrong measures. In an organization, different sets of measures are used for different levels of review, but all measures should lead towards some desired final output result. Nothing should be measured for the sake of measurement; if it's worth measuring, it's worth reviewing. An unreviewed measure dies as surely as an unwatered plant.

Also ask the questions that define *your* job — what do people need you to do to help them do what they need to do. If you don't ask, you rely on guesswork to determine whether you are dealing with the most important problems. Doing the wrong thing well is worse when managers do it because the leverage for causing permanent damage is higher.

If progress is reviewed regularly (both in formal reviews and in the hallway), using the right set of measures and asking the right questions, the probability is good that you'll get the results you want even if a poor job of defining desired results and priorities is done initially. Consistently asking the right questions gives people a vehicle for knowing exactly what results are expected.

Now that how to get and keep only the best people and how to make clear to them what needs to be done have been discussed, let's go on to how to let them do what needs to be done.

LETTING THEM DO WHAT NEEDS TO BE DONE

CHAPTER 25

HOW TO LET
THEM DO IT

N OW THAT you have the right people and they know exactly what needs to be done, the next step is to let them do it. That gives *them* job ownership and it gives *you* time to work on the problems that only you can solve. Your job is to review (by asking the right questions), to advise (mostly on request), and to work on problems above people's pay grade (such as making systems work). To let them do it, take three specific actions:

1. Make clear who is responsible for what.

2. Attach authority to responsibility — get the decision-making process as close to the work as possible.

3. Develop useful information and make it readily available.

Each of these actions will be dealt with in a separate chapter. But how do they lead to job ownership? (If you know how they work, they can be modified when needed.) These three actions give the following results:

People get a chance to succeed — and fail — on their own. There is no better training in the world. They learn how to do the things they are responsible for without needing your constant input. You can concentrate on fixing the failures and letting the successes run.

Motivation comes from doing "noble work," making real decisions and exercising real authority. This is the ultimate turn-on. Think about when you first got some real authority and went out and actually exercised it.

The amount of time spent transferring information so it can be reported to a higher level is reduced dramatically. The people who know the data can report it to the next higher level themselves. There's no need to pass information up the organization chain through particular channels. If the person who's in charge of that piece of data really has authority, everyone who needs the information and needs something done about it can go directly to him or her. Like a data base computer system, the data is entered only once at one place and everybody goes there to get it.

Clear lines of responsibility and authority make it easy to know where to focus resources to solve problems. Don't distribute authority to fit some theory of participative management; do it in a way that's productive. When people know what to do and have the authority to do it, the nonperformers stand out vividly. There's no one else to blame. Good people are very productive when they work this way, and they can tell precisely where to apply resources to fix problems.

The next chapter discusses how to implement each of these actions in a way that gets results in a matrix management organization — an excellent example of a system in which success depends largely on letting good people do what they know needs to be done.

CHAPTER 26

MATRIX MANAGEMENT ORGANIZATIONS —THEORY AND REALITY

THE ACTIONS discussed in the previous chapter (make clear who is responsible for what; attach authority to responsibility — get the decision-making process as close to the work as possible; and develop useful information that is readily available to everyone) can keep a matrix management organization in balance. This type of organization will be used as a framework for discussing the implementation of these actions in the following chapters.

MATRIX MANAGEMENT ORGANIZATIONS — THE THEORY

Matrix management organizations superimpose program management over an organization with conventional manufacturing, engineering, and service functions. A program management organization markets programs to the outside world and buys from each function the resources to perform the programs. The end results are efficiencies associated with centralized functions plus the concentrated attention to move a program through the various stages of engineering and manufacturing — ideally, the best of both worlds.

Each program manager competes for the resources necessary to do their job. The program office does not supervise anyone in engineering or manufacturing directly, but each of these functions assigns people to work with the program office to help focus resources as necessary to keep programs on schedule and budget. Essentially, these people have two bosses — the functional managers who pay their salary and the program office. If they satisfy both, matrix management works well.

The Japanese recognized the potential usefulness of this arrangement. In 1953, Konosuke Matsushita, founder of the corporation that bears his name, organized his divisions into product groups with division managers who reported to the president of Matsushita and the group vice-presidents who were product group specialists. His comment was that we all grow up under two bosses — our parents — and it is the nature of life to balance competing demands that arise from such arrangements. The advantages of resource sharing and flexibility outweigh the problems if the proper balance is kept. In his view, balance is all.

The key to matrix management *is* balance — the balance of responsibilities. Ideally, only the program offices and the people in functions who are assigned specific program responsibilities focus on programs. Everyone else works primarily to optimize functional performance. Functional managers focus on people, methods, measures, and systems. Their primary job is the continual improvement of the processes used to produce their products and services. They think *function*, not program; *process*, not product. They discharge their program responsibilities by carefully selecting and training the people in their functions who they assign to programs, by supporting these people adequately and resolving issues that concern the priority use of functional resources by different programs. Otherwise, functional managers concentrate on the function.

This functional concentration results in products and services with the best possible combination of quality, cost, and delivery — Productive Quality. As they extract these products and services via matrix management, the program offices sell and deliver them successfully in the program orientation their customers want. The gain is a whole greater than the sum of its parts. This is the theory, which is definitely achievable; however, the reality is often different.

MATRIX MANAGEMENT ORGANIZATIONS — THE REALITY

Functional managers must concentrate on creating an efficient function. But where are they driven to spend most of their time? What single issue absorbs more of their working hours than any other issue? It's that old devil "program status." The majority of function managers' time is not spent getting the best people, or making clear to them what needs to be done, or creating systems in which they can do it. It's not used on the three steps that will determine how well the functions, which they are paid to manage, will perform. The biggest slice of time is spent being a deputy program manager. Program and functional responsibilities are out of balance.

Even worse, the curse rubs off on everyone who works for them. "The pace of the boss is the pace of the gang." If programs drive the boss, programs drive the entire organization. Functional problems are addressed in the time left over from working on program problems. The tail wags the dog. It takes a determined and courageous manager to set things right.

THE INFORMATION TRANSFER CHAIN

The information transfer chain is a symptom of the balance problem and a great time destroyer. The chain starts with weekly program reviews (often held on Fridays) between top management and the program managers. This means the manufacturing/engineering managers hold preparatory meetings on Thursdays; individual department/laboratory managers, on Wednesdays; next level management meets Tuesdays; ad infinitum.

The purpose of these meetings is to give status on programs and to find the problems affecting cost and schedule. The attendees are people having something to do with performance on part of the program. Since the business is program-oriented, this is a long list. Everyone holding a meeting wants the highest level person in their area at the meeting. The inevitable result is that a lot of people spend time

151

getting briefed for, sitting in, and getting debriefed from a lot of meetings.

The chain is driven by the expectation that everyone should know about key program problems, the plan to fix them, and the progress being made on the plan; everyone helps the program manager do their job. Functional managers must kill this assumption. If it is killed successfully, they can get to work on their real jobs.

WHY IS THE REALITY AS IT IS?

If matrix management is so efficient when it's balanced properly, why does it get unbalanced? Who crowns the program manager as king? The answer, as is so often the case, is that everyone does.

Program issues have all the attributes of show business: talking about the ins and outs of a technical problem is fun; also, a strong feeling of accomplishment — and lots of organizational rewards — are involved when you participate in a weekend crash effort to get hardware fixed in time to prevent a crisis. You receive immediate positive feedback. It's a lot more fun than wrestling with the problem of getting capital approved to build another solder station — or improving the system for processing capital appropriations.

Program review meetings invariably fall behind schedule because the assembled managers — often years away from their days of being technical experts and/or project managers — and having had only a few minutes to think about the new technical problem, begin to wander into the swamp of talking about redesigning the system. The fact that engineers by the roomful, together with the vendor and customer experts who have been called in, are working on the problem down in the bowels of the organization, doesn't deter the assembled managers. It's a lot more fun to talk about a design problem than it is to try to improve program performance by grinding through ways to make systems more responsive to the people who work in them.

These meetings fall into a catch-22 category: The only thing worse than going to the meeting is not being invited (and, thus, falling out of the inner circle). If you don't know the latest disaster on the XYZ program, you must not be at the level that really counts. It indeed takes a courageous and determined functional manager to say that's not where he or she can contribute the most.

An effective functional manager concentrates on getting a better yield at the solder station or improving the system that controls engineering change orders so response time can be reduced below the normal human lifespan. Programs always have some new glitch to resolve — but if functional managers are successful in changing the processes they're working on, they could change the way the company does business for the next decade (and potential glitches in hundreds of future programs).

Clearly, the problem is one of balance. Top management has to reward functional managers who improve their functions in the same way they reward program managers who solve a program crisis. Program managers make a lot of money and have a lot of authority — as it should be because of the responsibility; they are producing today's revenue. But the company will not succeed in the long run unless it also has people thinking process rather than program. Truly, balance is all.

HOW TO ACHIEVE BALANCE

Assume you are a functional manager who plans to implement the actions that will restore balance to matrix management. Begin by making clear who is responsible for what. For the company to succeed, functional management has to run the function well. The concept is that your job is to run a function through which programs can flow easily. Your job should not be (as it often is when systems are not balanced) to work on a list of programs and get them through the function you happen to be in. The people who head program teams are responsible for program decisions and everyone has to support them accordingly — that's the implicit understanding that makes matrix management work. But as a functional manager, your job is to build successful functions. That's what you are *responsible* for.

153

Focus on improving the function. Develop job measures on a functional basis (most aerospace measures are on a program basis) to have a baseline for improvement. Every program should flow through the function with minimum cost and schedule. Cooperate in every way to help the people responsible for program performance, but measure your success based on functional performance.

The people to emulate are the program managers. They expend energy getting functions to give priority to and to perform well on their programs. They cooperate in every way they can to get that edge but measure themselves entirely on how well their program meets planned budget and schedule. They'll work to increase the yield on their own programs and if that helps increase the yield for everyone, that's nice. But they can't worry about yield problems on others' programs. Their responsibility is their own program and they're not going to do your job for you. They're going to concentrate on program problems. They've got the responsibility issue just right.

Get the issue right for your function. Except for the people who are assigned to programs, no one should act as a deputy program manager. You are responsible for the performance of the *function*. Do your job — not someone else's. The people you assign, functional *program* people, have to get the same direction. Their responsibility is to get that program through the function on schedule and in budget. It's not their job to patch up the function. If your functional performance is lousing up their program, you need to know where the problems are so they can be fixed. You'll be glad to get suggestions on *how* to do it. But it's your job. Everybody is going to cooperate, but everybody is going to do *their* job.

Having made clear who is responsible for what, the next action is to distribute authority so functional program people can do their job and the rest of the team can run the function. The functional program people deal with the program office and they have the authority to act. You don't need to be briefed constantly on the transfer of information up or down. You have more time to improve the function because of no longer sitting in meetings with program office

154

people, reviewing all the programs they are working on. Work program issues only when functional program people need your involvement. (Yes, you need good functional program people in the functions to make this work — get and keep only the best, remember?) On the occasions when people do ask for help, you can do something for them because you're not tied up reviewing the status of everything. Train yourself to say those terrible words, "I don't know," about program issues and refer questions to program office people.

A special note needs to be made here about bidding for new business and making make/buy decisions. Function managers need to be actively involved in these issues. Yes, program managers come to you on a program basis, but functional knowledge is needed to respond. By concentrating on running your function, you know the current capabilities (and shortcomings) and that makes it much easier to make those new bids on the products and services. Make/buy issues can be addressed knowledgeably because trade-offs can be made, based on hard data about how your function works. Worrying about the progress of existing programs and bidding new programs by "gut feel" makes it nearly impossible to do either job well.

Attaining this ideal world to work in is, of course, hard to realize. You help make it hard if you have difficulty giving up authority over people and letting them take directions from someone else. To give them authority to do things as your surrogate is easy, but it's harder to give them authority to act at the direction of someone else (like the program office). That, however, is the essence of matrix management. The degree to which authority is distributed determines whether matrix management will work as it's intended to work — effectively moving programs through well-managed functions. It's a win-win situation if done right.

Giving people the authority to make decisions also requires giving them access to key operating information so they can make *informed* decisions. Which brings us to the last action: Creating systems that make information readily available to everyone can cut costs and frustration.

Functions tend to hold information tight to their chest. They get "help" from the program office when good news reserves and/or bad news problems develop, so they manage the release of their information. Similarly, the program office keeps, essentially, several sets of books; a different set for customers, management, and functional suppliers. Program managers believe that if the functions know the real schedule and cost details, they will not work hard enough or save enough money. If customers or management see certain information too soon, the program manager also gets unwanted "help." Guarding this information and releasing it in strategic pieces takes an army of cost analysis people and a great deal of management time.

Creating data systems that make general information available to everyone eliminates the need for an army of data protectors and for spending a lot of management time searching for the "real" data. Decisions can be made close to the work because everyone must have real facts to work with. This recommendation sounds straightforward but is a major cultural change. *Trust* people to make intelligent use of the "real" information. This emphasizes the need for having only the best people who know exactly what to do. Giving them the available data is a key step in letting them do it.

EFFECTIVE FUNCTIONS ARE THE FOUNDATION OF A MATRIX ORGANIZATION

The company with the most effective functional management will have the most effective matrix management. Program managers who know they are getting the lowest total cost for what their customers need can concentrate on the program without perceiving the need for a lot of mini-program managers. Without good functions, system crises are worked on only as they occur, with the primary goal of getting a specific program past a specific point. With this approach, the problems that occur this year on this program will happen next year on the next program. When you concentrate on understanding and controlling functions, you can operate with an expectation of being able to predict reasonably well what each function can do and what that means for each program. You find a baseline for continual improvement. There is balance — and control of your business.

THE WORD IS BALANCE — NOT ABANDONMENT

There's one caveat to discuss before moving on. The stress is on a *balance* of responsibilities — not abandonment. Functional managers should not play Pontius Pilate and wash their hands of program problems. The issue is to balance program and functional responsibilities — not to dump one for the other. The program office is normally the customer of the functions in matrix management and the customer must always have proper service. The best service is provided by a well-run function and systems with capabilities which meet the program manager's needs. That function and those systems are obtained by balancing responsibilities, just as matrix management succeeds by balancing organizational responsibilities.

The next three chapters go into detail about how to implement each of the actions just discussed (make clear who is responsible for what; attach authority to responsibility; develop useful information that is readily available to everyone) and show how to solve problems similar to that of balancing matrix management. Making it *possible* for people to do what needs to be done is how to get the payoff from getting and keeping only the best people and making clear to them what needs to be done.

CHAPTER 27

MAKING CLEAR
WHO IS RESPONSIBLE FOR
WHAT

SECTION III talked about the need to define the job in large enough terms — people should do the "whole job." But to permit people to do what needs to be done, you must make clear who is responsible for what so they can concentrate properly. You *do* want them to do the whole job, but to do it in the areas they are responsible for.

Encourage people to cooperate, care, and work primarily to make the company succeed — because that's how they succeed individually. But no one can do everything and trying to makes it impossible to do anything well. Don't diffuse your people's efforts by making them feel vaguely responsible for everything. Concentration and focus makes everyone effective. When you make clear what people are and are *not* responsible for, they are free to concentrate — and succeed.

THE RESPONSIBILITY OF OPERATING
FUNCTIONS IS TO OPERATE

The operating functions (engineering, manufacturing, and marketing) have the basic responsibilities to design, build, and market the products and services to which the company owes its existence. If these functions don't perform, there is no company. Support the operating functions or you won't survive.

The previous chapter on matrix management has examples of the problems involved in getting operating functions to agree on who is responsible for what so the proper balance between program and functional responsibilities can be struck. There are many other areas where engineering, manufacturing, and marketing can — and do — get into conflicts. Most often these are battles about who knows *best* how to do what needs to be done (what I call the "who's in charge here?" issue). They agree their responsibility is to operate — they just have different opinions on how best to do it.

Although these battles can generate friction, they do not represent the biggest operational problem. If you work in the way described in this book, the battles can be resolved with good faith negotiations and Productive Quality can be achieved. All three functions *do* focus on their key responsibility — operating.

The biggest problem concerning responsibility comes when the role of service functions is not made clear (and/or they don't pay enough to get capable people). This problem creates a drag on the operating functions and is the cause of the biggest loss of productivity. When the service functions do not provide the service they are responsible for, it is impossible for the operating functions to run well. The constant battle of who is supposed to do what takes precedence over how best to do it. Solving the question of service functions' responsibility is crucial to letting people do what needs to be done.

THE RESPONSIBILITY OF SERVICE FUNCTIONS IS TO PROVIDE SERVICE

Service functions do not produce a saleable product. They would not exist without the operating functions, but this does not make them unimportant. Quite the contrary — they have a very important job. The job of a service function is to provide service to the operating functions, helping them operate as efficiently as possible. Their job does *not* include making demands on the operating functions. Their job is to *ease* the burden of the operating functions, not to make it harder to carry.

Be sure service functions do not see their job as completing forms in "accordance with procedure" and/or developing and defending the procedures themselves. Then the tail wags the dog. If existing procedures force service functions to provide service ineffectively (the operating functions, as the *customers* of the service, are the only judges of whether that service is being provided effectively), then the service functions must lead the charge to change the procedures. Their job is not to defend existing procedures. Their job is to adopt procedures that permit them to provide the service the operating functions need. Make clear the role of the service functions and *measure them accordingly.* Otherwise they will not be able to provide the service for which they are responsible or find a baseline for improving their performance.

WHEN SERVICE IS FORGOTTEN

The example list is endless. The quality assurance inspector who sees the job as a hurdle for manufacturing to leap before the product goes to the customer rather than being the point man who gets it through customer source inspection. The buyer who sees the job as ensuring the auditable stack of paper is filled out properly, instead of being the person responsible to show manufacturing how to get parts at the lowest total cost. The financial analyst who sees the job as "protecting the revenue" rather than as a resource person who helps explain financial problems and the options to fix them.

One critical area is the staff service functions where policies and procedures that define operating methods are written. The intent is to insure that operating functions perform in accordance with company and customer (especially government) requirements. Some policies must be followed consistently or, in the extreme cases, people end up going to jail. Large corporations, have need for staffs (very small) to insure that they operate properly. But the key test of the staff's effectiveness is whether they do this job as a service or as a police force.

If staff functions see their role as *service* functions, they write procedures in the most flexible way to help operations run as effectively as possible within company and customer restraints. The operating functions define what is effective, and the service functions try to modify procedures continually to help the operating functions.

A substantial problem exists if staff functions see their role as police protecting both company and customer from the devious operating functions. The procedures become the product of the staff functions and the concept of service disappears. The staff functions write procedures that comply with company and customer requirements (as interpreted by the staff functions), and see their role as policing these documents, and forcing the operating functions to follow them "or else." This drives up costs substantially. The operations run inefficiently, trying to get around procedures that don't work, and procedure audits become high-cost nightmares.

The irony of this situation is that the need to pass audits is often stated as the reason for staff functions forcing procedures down the throat of the functions. The most common audit problem, failing to do what procedures say is done, happens most often when staff functions *control* the procedure-writing process. If the operating functions have *real approval* (responsibly exercised) on what is written and the staff functions write as a service, then procedures that satisfy the basic policies *and* work in the real world are found. Systems reached jointly will be followed because they are responsive and they work. Then, you can focus primarily on the *adequacy* of systems — an issue resolved much more easily than that of failing to follow system documents.

When the documents aren't followed, a lack of control over what happens on the floor is felt. That's a major problem for everyone. When the documents are at least followed consistently, then the main problem to resolve is differences between the intent of company and customer requirements and the intent of the documents. Solutions can be negotiated within the comfort zone of everyone — everyone is confident that they know what happens on the floor. Thus, even from a narrow-minded "let's be sure we pass the audit" view, the best approach is for the staff functions to write procedures as an ex-

161

pert service for operations, who have the authority for final approval.

In summary, letting people do what needs to be done requires service functions to see their job as providing the kind of support described in this chapter. Operations do not need to know what they *can't* do — that's an ever-growing and, essentially, useless list. They expect service functions to be the experts in knowing the rules and to provide service in accordance with them. If the service is considered poor by their customers in the operating functions, and if the service functions feel the reason for the poor service stems directly from the procedures, then the service functions should take the lead in trying to fix the problem. The situation should not be left as something else the operating functions has to live with.

Certainly this requires the ultimate in cooperation between the service and operating functions. Sometimes both must select among undesirable alternatives so that rules can be followed and effective operation achieved. It requires, in short, that managers from the CEO down act in a managerial way. But, first it requires that the responsibility of service functions is made clear. They can't respond properly if what needs to be done is not defined properly. If the operating functions are to do what they are responsible for, they need the *freedom* to work only on the problems they are responsible for; the responsibilities of all other functions have to be made clear so the operating function is supported accordingly.

GOOD SERVICE COMES FROM GOOD PEOPLE

The responsibilities of service functions must be defined because that is usually the crux of the problem — people are doing the wrong thing as well as they can. Sometimes the problem is cumulative. If the service function believes its job is to fill out the forms, it hires people who are capable of doing only that because they are cheaper. People are accumulated who aren't capable of doing the whole job, even if finally defined properly. Like every other function, service functions have to follow the three steps and they should spend enough to get only the best. There is no room for the attitude that the best are hired for operations while service functions are expected to perform with people at lower average salaries. Providing service *properly* is a very difficult job and only the best people can do it well. Good companies have service functions that provide service.

Once it is made clear who is responsible for what, the next step is to distribute authority to people to match their responsibility. That's the subject of the next chapter.

CHAPTER 28

ATTACHING AUTHORITY TO RESPONSIBILITY

GET DECISIONS MADE
AS CLOSE TO THE WORK AS POSSIBLE

ATTACHING authority to responsibility is an old cliché, but it's rarely practiced in pure form. A lot of "authority" is subject to constant review in a cycle of checks and balances. Getting a decision made requires jumping over a series of hurdles. Many of these hurdles are put up by people "protecting the company," but some reflect well-meant attempts to help less experienced people avoid unintended bad decisions. A better method would be to put more energy into training and development so people can learn to act responsibly. Knock down the hurdles. Make it possible for decisions to be made *now* by the people responsible for performing. That's how to keep processes moving. Waiting is waste. Avoid waiting by distributing authority throughout the operation.

Equally important, people close to the work know better than anyone what makes their work difficult and what changes would make it easier. Operating systems should take advantage of that knowledge. Base decisions about how to create and change systems on what the people close to the work tell you. Have them define the best way to implement company policies. They should make decisions that concern how to keep the work moving and decisions on which services to buy from a central function and which to perform themselves. Often all of these decisions are made by people far away from the work (usually in a central function). That's a sure recipe for systems that are not responsive, and, in terms of *total* cost, systems that are the most costly.

164

THE REAL HIDDEN PLANT

A lot of effort has been made in recent years to reduce the costs of the so-called *hidden plant* (scrap, rework, and repair — or SR^2). These costs are real and worth reducing. But another hidden plant fits the term much better — with a cost far exceeding that of SR^2; a cost that can be measured directly in terms of excess people ("costs walk on two legs") and indirectly in terms of delay and frustration.

The real hidden plant is the one housing the "system beaters." These are people whose job is to do what cannot be done in a reasonable time or at a reasonable cost by going through the "system." Their job is to beat the system and get the work done. The ground rule is that it is much easier to apologize for beating the system after the problem has been solved than it is to apologize for not getting the problem solved because the system doesn't work.

This is the world of expeditors who hand-carry everything, petty cash purchases that violate the spirit if not the letter of the law, and records that are kept by hand or on personal computers because the central system is too slow or can't be trusted. It is the world of professional personnel with purposely vague job titles who write computer programs, do training, develop processes, and do facility layouts because the "central" functions charged with these responsibilities move with glacial slowness far up in staff heaven. The distance of the central function from the work is so great that often their output is not useful for the organization even when it is finally delivered.

The worst of all possible worlds is in this hidden plant. Systems do not get fixed because they are bypassed and the problems they cause are not brought to light. The end result is bearing the cost of both the central functions and the system beaters and expensive delays caused by nonresponsive systems. Locating the decision-making process far from where the work is being done is a prime cause of the hidden plant.

One reason the hidden plant is perpetuated is the misperception that the economies of scale of central functions and the security of multiple signatures save the company money (a "second signature" approach generally does save money — it's the third through the twentieth signature that creates negative returns). These "savings" don't begin to cover the costs of the system beaters, not to mention the loss of initiative and creativity from trying to work through non-responsive systems.

It's better to have decisions made close to the work and to fix procedural problems after the fact than to create systems that try to insure that no procedural mistakes will be made. A system insuring no such mistakes also insures that nothing can be done in minimal total time and at minimal total cost. At bottom, people have to be trusted. With trust, decisions can be made close to the work and systems can be made to work. The best way to eliminate system beaters is to have systems that don't need to be beat.

Trust is essential to letting people do what needs to be done. It requires good people who are well trained and have a clear direction about what needs to be done. It requires, in short, everything discussed in the first three sections of the book. Then the actions that allow people to do what needs to be done can be implemented.

Even in an environment with the proper sense of trust, functions are often centralized because standardization is confused with centralization — it's assumed that centralization leads to standardization. But the *benefits* of standardization can be obtained without centralization by developing broadly defined standard systems that are meant to be tailored by the specific operation that uses them. This is the lowest total cost approach, and it stems directly from the premise that people need the necessary authority to make decisions close to the work.

DISTRIBUTE AUTHORITY TO BUILD AN OPERATION WITH DECISIONS MADE CLOSE TO THE WORK

Distributing authority means giving it to the people who need it to do the jobs defined for them. Don't just delegate it for specific cases at specific times for specific purposes. Give people the authority you would want to have if you had their job. Stretch signature delegation policies to the limit. People should be able to act. Take the risk that some people will purposely misuse the authority and /or not be able to handle it. The benefits from people who make proper use of authority will far outweigh the problems caused by those who don't (especially as those who don't disappear with the bottom 10%).

Many have heard about the supervisor who is told he or she has substantial responsibility and is an important member of the management team. The words are nice, but when the supervisor discovers it takes two signature levels above theirs to buy an eight-dollar can of paint, they understandably wonder how much action they can take on their own initiative. Many of these horror stories are caused by the "protect-the-company" use of multiple signatures on any document that dispenses company funds. The money lost from misuse of signature authority is a fraction of the amount lost waiting for multiple signatures to be gathered. Incremental savings decline exponentially beyond the second signature, while the cost of collection goes up at the same rate. The solution is to keep required signatures as close to two — and as close to those requesting the funds — as possible. Trust, again.

Often, it's not fair to criticize the people who insist on the multiple signatures. They're measured on the loss of funds, not on the time of service or the total cost of putting up hurdles. They respond accordingly. This is another example of the need to measure service organizations on the quality of the service they provide, as discussed in the previous chapter. If someone is capable of being responsible, then they're capable of being trusted with authority. The company doesn't need protection from them.

AVOID MICROMANAGING
THE USE OF AUTHORITY

Be involved only where you need to be involved. Demonstrate to people that you are serious about the distribution of authority and their freedom to use it. The litmus test is the degree to which people can interact with peers and superiors without feeling the need to get approval ahead of time. If it's what's needed to do their job, they should feel free to go ahead on their own, regardless of what level they deal with. That's what exercising authority means.

Anytime you say something like "be sure I see anything that goes to Mr. X (usually your boss)" you are falling into the micromanaging trap. People should use the authority given to them. Only get involved when asked for advice — *they* should decide on your involvement, not you. They have to learn when they need your input. It's okay to say you don't know about the XYZ issue when your boss brings it up if that responsibility has been given to one of your people. If this approach is used consistently, people will learn to talk to each other directly rather than using you as a message carrier. So much the better.

The peer/superior issue is usually the problem. There is little difficulty in letting people below your level resolve problems without your input. But there is a nagging need to know what's going on with peers and superiors. If authority has been truly distributed, you don't need to know. Depend on people to bring forward any problems they can't handle (that's why you spend so much time getting and keeping only the best people). Avoid micromanaging in this situation, and it can be avoided anywhere.

MANAGING BY EXCEPTION — YOUR EXCEPTION

Managing by exception sounds good, but it often means reviewing the status of everything people are working on and focusing on items that are in trouble. A better approach is to review only items of specific interest to you plus those your people want to bring up. Everything else can be handled by your people. If neither you nor they feel the need to review it, why waste time talking about it?

Spend your energy on what is best done by you — generally above other people's pay grade. Don't concern yourself with day-to-day problems unless people bring them forward for your help. Stay out of ongoing information transfer loops (briefings, meetings, memos, etc.) that are involved with day-to-day problems. You have more important things to do with your time. After having worked on all the day-to-day issues earlier in your career, you have little to gain from continuing to work them. Focus on futures. Eliminate those things that keep you from the futures — and the information transfer loop is one of those things. Eliminate it by distributing authority.

Operations should be as self-sufficient as possible. In a sense, that is exactly what happens when authority is distributed. The operation is broken into the smallest possible piece — an individual person. Make that person as self-sufficient as possible by giving them as much authority as possible; build an operation by putting together groups of people who have as much authority and self-sufficiency as can be given to them. The chain they follow to reach the place where a decision can be made should be as short as possible. Part of self-sufficiency includes the determining whether to use centralized services. The productive effect of operations that control their own destiny far outweighs the alleged economies of scale of *dictated* centralized services.

CENTRALIZE BY ASKING THE PEOPLE WHO USE THE SERVICE

Centralization for certain functions and services certainly has its advantages. The question is whether services are performed within the organization or through central services. This argument has been going on for at least the last 200 years or so — depending on which date is selected as the beginning of the industrial revolution. Here is a simple way to settle the argument for any operation. Centralized staff functions are service functions. Their customers are line operations. Get the best results by asking the customers what services they want centralized and what services they want to do themselves.

If line operations agree they want a certain service provided centrally, you can be sure they will use that service and not create duplicates on their own. If a service is centralized that the line operations want to provide on their own, you are simply creating a hidden plant. In addition to letting the line operations decide what services they want centralized, let the line operations decide how much service they want. They should have a strong input into the size of the budget for each central function. Some functions must be centralized at the insistence of the outside customer and government regulation, and these can be budgeted as musts even before talking to line operations about their requirements. Beyond using centralized services where outside forces dictate, the services provided should be no larger or more costly than the operations are willing to pay for.

The last step in letting everyone do what needs to be done and the subject of the next chapter is making sure they have the information they need to operate effectively.

CHAPTER 29

DEVELOPING USEFUL INFORMATION THAT IS READILY AVAILABLE TO EVERYONE

DATA IS JUST THE BEGINNING

PEOPLE need information (which begets knowledge which begets wisdom) to make decisions. Data is the source of most information, but data rarely yields information directly. Converting data to information and making it available is an important part of letting people do what needs to be done. This is accomplished by: developing the capability to convert data to useful information; making that information available to everyone (especially people close to the work); focusing on the analysis of readily available data to get information rather than expending excessive resources to get data in multiple formats; and making the data reflect what is actually happening. Each of these actions will be discussed in this chapter.

CONVERTING DATA TO INFORMATION IS A SPECIAL SKILL

Converting data to information takes people who have both the training and inclination to do so. Teasing the nuggets of information out of data and presenting them so they are clear to everyone is an art. Hiring people with this kind of talent is the most productive way to meet changing information needs. A simple data collection system with intelligence behind it is much more effective than complex systems that attempt to provide for the analysis of all possible cuts of data. Without the people to provide that intelligence, data collection resources are wasted.

Many companies need people whose full-time job is to find out what information is needed, determine the data from which the information can be derived, and convert the data into the required information. These people range from MBAs to self-made people, close to the work, who know what's needed to improve productivity based on their knowledge of the process. A team (as few as two people make a team) of both types often works best. The emphasis has to be on analysis — collecting data is straightforward compared to knowing how to make proper use of it.

INFORMATION HAS TO BE DISTRIBUTED AS WIDELY AS POSSIBLE TO BE USEFUL

There's an old cliché to the effect that money is like manure — if spread around wisely it can produce a lot of growth, but if piled up in one place it begins to stink. The same is true of information. Reports, representing lots of preparation dollars, end up merely filling three-ring binders in someone's bookcase. One problem is that these reports are often full of data rather than information. But even if the data-to-information conversion process has been well done, the information often doesn't get distributed beyond the meeting at which it's presented.

Get the information out where it can do the most good — to the people who are close to the work. They can act most directly on the information, and the feedback they provide helps in the process of converting data to information. Too often the information is presented to management only. The people close to the work not only have difficulty getting the information they need, they get burdened with providing data for functions like finance and the program office (and then don't get to see information based on that data). National security and company privacy limits must be observed, but beyond those limits make information available to everyone.

THE PAYOFF IS IN DATA ANALYSIS, NOT COLLECTION

The corollary to committing resources to data analysis is to strive for simplicity in data collection. The 80/20 rule applies in a unique way here. Eighty percent of the information can be obtained by expending only 20% of the cost of trying to collect enough data to get 100% of the desired information. Also, often the direction data collecting should take is not known until some data is collected and analysis done. The more complex the collection process, the harder it is to change when initial analysis indicates that different data should be collected.

Many attempts to collect data that could yield useful information never get off the ground because of overkilling the front end of the process. When great effort is expended defining the data to collect, collecting the data becomes so difficult that the project simply expires. It's better to start simply by using readily available data and concentrating on analysis to get useful information. After learning the cause-and-effect levers, you can derive the information directly or define incremental data that is easily collected and will give the necessary incremental information.

A symptom of the data collection problem burdens most operating functions: the demand by other functions for data in formats different from those existing in operations. The result is that operations are requested to provide data in many different forms. This puts the burden in the wrong place. Operations should only collect data to get operating information. If functions such as the program office, finance, and human resources want data in some other form, they should figure out how to translate the operating information into that form. Operations already has enough to do and needs to expend resources on analysis that tells them how to improve productivity — not on collecting and providing data they have no use for.

Make all functions responsible for their own data analysis as an incentive to get agreement to the concept that all data is available to everyone (the data must reflect what is actually going on). Functions holding data have to provide it in any form requested. If it's available to all (and if it's reliable data), then other functions are expected to do their own analysis from the data as it already exists. Making everyone responsible for their own analysis helps develop the iterative process of learning how to get the information needed for improvement. This development happens most effectively when people focus on data analysis rather than data collection, but it requires data that reflects what is actually going on — the fourth step.

THE DATA MUST REFLECT WHAT IS ACTUALLY GOING ON

Developing a system that will provide useful information is impossible with bad or missing data. But people can become reluctant to provide reliable data (or any data) unless the organizational atmosphere is such that:

1. The data they provide does not result in an endless series of callers who want explanations about real or perceived problems in the data; *one* review session for those concerned should be enough. Otherwise, inevitably people who provide the data avoid making problems clear until they are ready to take the time to discuss them at length. That means bad data, bad information, and bad decisions.

2. All data (except that which affects security) is available to anyone. It is too valuable to be held by any one person or function. Having access to all the data gives people an incentive for providing their piece. It also prevents the reinvention of the wheel. Books do not need to be cooked and turf does not need to be defended. Anyone can know what is happening in any area, and no function has to hold data until they are ready to feed it into the world a piece at a time. Data is truly community property.

Operating this way will free people whose prime task is to prepare, review, and revise data until each successive manager feels comfortable about releasing it. In many organizations, just enough data is published to meet minimums, and several back-up books are kept to "explain" each item to a given inquisitor. (These explanations are like those used to "explain" changes in the stock market — the same rationale suffices to explain an increase or decrease. It all depends on whether you're buying or selling.) Eliminating this sort of record keeping substantially increases productivity. Fewer people are needed, frustration is decreased, and reliable data is created.

Creating an organization in which people have open access to data is a *very* difficult thing to do. It takes restraint that increases substantially going up successive management levels. You need good data, and all the data. *If it's used for ad hoc inquisitions you will not get it.* Give managers the opportunity to manage, based on the information gained from open access to all the data, and remember, if people must spend their time explaining data rather than working on problems, they will stop providing the data. It's a very vicious circle.

Resist the urge to micromanage. You do not have to respond instantly to questions on every piece of data to satisfy the doubts of every observer. That attitude creates a self-defeating process. Not only are the managers not allowed to manage, it insures that the data containing insights into problems will dry up. To be assured that information remains available, use it carefully. This is surely the place to apply the analogy of not killing the goose that lays the golden eggs. Keep those eggs coming. Good data is precious and must be handled with care. Make the reward system reward those managers who are open with their data.

THE PROGRAM OFFICE
VERSUS THE OPERATING FUNCTIONS

One of the worst examples of the misuse of data can occur between program offices and operating functions in matrix management (see Matrix Management Organizations — Theory and Reality, page 149). The program offices negotiate budgets with the operating functions, based on the cost estimates submitted by operating functions during the bidding process. Initial negotiations are followed by multiple cost-to-complete negotiations until the program is over. In a bad situation, there is constant data warfare between the program offices and the operating functions. A typical bad scenario goes as follows:

During the bidding process, with outside customers, the program offices push for the lowest possible estimates to assure winning the bid. The operating functions also want to win, but they have to do the work when the program is awarded. They want to make cost estimates that give them a reasonable chance to do what they said they could do. They know their performance reviews are going to hang on how well they perform on the subsequent budgets they get from the program office.

Both groups operate under a heavy cloud of cynicism. The program office suspects that the operating functions pads their bids, and expends substantial effort trying to find and eliminate the pads. They can quote chapter and verse from programs where underruns were larger than the margins by which other programs were lost. They talk constantly about competitors who do everything faster and with fewer people than the operating functions they are forced to work with.

The operating functions have heard it all before. The program office has urged them to make rock-bottom bids for the sake of the company, the country, and the free world. With the same assurance that accompanies "the check is in the mail," operating functions have been told that when budgets are issued the program office will recognize that this is really a rock-bottom bid, they will take into ac-

176

count the fact that the design is still on the back of an envelope, and they will adjust fairly for things given away during price negotiations. Each operating manager has responded at least once to such pleas — the result was that their budget was cut just as much as that of the guys who really did have pads. For the rest of the program, they remember clearly, they attended bloody program reviews where their character, ancestry, competence, and future with the company were strongly questioned.

Being rational people, the operating functions prefer not to live that way. Their bids inevitably grow conservative (which they assume will offset cuts from the program office when budgets are issued and, thus, everyone will start from the proper baseline). Their people are instructed not to release any cost data before the manager has seen it and is satisfied that he or she is ready to expend the energy to defend it in its present form (which may or may not reflect what is actually happening in the operation).

For the program office the cost-estimating process becomes a hunt for the hidden pad — where is it and how big is it? It's a game that continues through rebids and ongoing estimates of cost-to-complete. The program office never wants to recognize cost increases, believing that aiming at a higher number will result in a higher number — they believe estimated costs become a self-fulfilling prophecy. Also, they don't want to acknowledge problems to the customer until the time is "right." The functions grow weary of doing estimates that are reduced by the program office on any pretext. They evolve to the frame of mind that says "tell me what number you want and I'll submit it"; they know the actuals will be the actuals at the end of the program — saying the numbers will be lower won't make them so.

This is a game that wastes a lot of energy. People feel forced to create, defend, and reconcile data rather than doing the work. The data itself becomes suspect. It becomes literally impossible to find "real" numbers that can be compared to the "original" budgets or be used as a baseline for making improvements. (The same effect happens in many audits or surveys or failure analyses — in short, in any situa-

177

tion where incentive to provide "real" data is limited because it simply hands the "enemy" a sword.)

The solution to the problem is *trust.* If everyone trusts everyone else to do what needs to be done in the best interest of the company, this kind of problem disappears. Easy to say, nearly impossible to do — although the problem is reduced in direct proportion to the number of good people working on each side, especially if those people know exactly what needs to be done and have the authority to do it. However difficult it is to create trust, make the effort to do it or you will always be dealing with suspect data. Every incremental effort made to reduce the level of game playing results in an incremental improvement in how things are done, moving you closer to the point where decisions are based on real data. It can't be said too often: *The data must reflect what is actually happening. Trust is the only elixir that works.*

PUTTING IT ALL TOGETHER

AND IN CONCLUSION . . .

I BELIEVE in one-page memos. They force selection of the key issues (if the issues can't be addressed on one page, they haven't been narrowed down sufficiently yet). One-pagers also get read (long memos end up in the folder to be read later — and "later" has a habit of becoming too late).

My passion for one-pagers was an ongoing joke in my group. When I told them I was taking a leave of absence to write this book, someone asked how many pages I thought the finished product would be. Immediately, someone shouted from the back of the room — "it's going to be a one-pager."

I couldn't keep the faith. This book is nearer 200 pages than one, but I want to keep at least the flavor of a one-pager in this conclusion. In less than 2,000 words, I'm going to summarize the key issues from the more than 50,000 words that have gone before. Public speaking gurus tell us to "tell them what you're going to tell them, tell them, tell them you've told them, then sit down." I've done the first two parts. Now I'm going to use this conclusion to tell everyone I've told them, and then I'm going to sit down.

THE BASIC PREMISE

No management approach can be guaranteed to be successful in all situations. You can look back at what successful companies have done, but their approaches are not necessarily translatable to other companies in other conditions, and, in fact, the same company often uses different approaches to succeed in different time frames. Sometimes the company ceases to be successful though it continues to use the same approach — circumstances change and the company doesn't.

However, every successful company or team takes three steps — regardless of the game plan they use. Using an operating philosophy — or framework — make it possible to accomplish these three steps in the real world you work in every day. Taking the following steps with that manage-

181

ment framework as a backdrop creates an organization capable of achieving Productive Quality, and that's what succeeds in today's world — and always has. A high level of quality or productivity alone is not good enough — it's the combination that beats the competition (the constant search to do things better at an affordable cost drives nearly all advances in our society).

THE THREE STEPS TO TAKE

1. Get and keep only the best people. (People are the most important variable in determining which organizations succeed and which fail.)

2. Make clear to them what needs to be done — define the job in terms of good performance and expected results.

3. Let them do it — create conditions in which they can do what needs to be done.

Many people have come to these same conclusions over the years, stated in various ways. The consistency with which they've been reached suggests strongly that they are the right conclusions. Having defined what you are trying to do, now focus on how to do it.

A LITTLE BIT AT A TIME ALL THE TIME

The framework for action is the philosophy "a little bit at a time, all the time." This is much harder to put into practice than to say, and it works only if pursued *all* the time. This approach takes the self-control to persist at something every day, the courage to plan for results over a long period of time, and the knowledge and intelligence to work steadily at defining everyone's job in terms of what they control. It is, however, a cumulative process and each small success makes it easier to get the next. Five concepts make up the process:

1. Any amount of effort is worthwhile if it is done all the time. Spending only 15 minutes a day doing something on a project accumulates into substantial results over time. Not doing anything today

because "there's not enough time" often results in not doing anything for months — one day at a time.

2. Learn by doing. Find the key issues by getting started and doing something — the key issues often turn out to be much different from what was thought before beginning. No amount of practice or planning can teach as much as actually doing something.

3. Start simple. Do *now* what can be done *now.* Waiting for the "grand design" prevents you from starting and learning.

4. No improvement is too small to implement. It's the cumulative effect of many small increments of compound interest that makes an IRA grow. You never know which incremental improvement in a system may lead to solutions to other problems thought to be unrelated.

5. The process has no end. All the time means *all* the time. It's what makes everything else work. The person who persists wins.

LEADING BEATS MANAGING

Your job is to lead. That means focusing on getting and keeping only the best people, making clear to them what needs to be done, and making it possible for *them* to do it. Depending on your people to do what needs to be done is how they get job ownership and how everyone succeeds.

A TOTAL QUALITY SAMPLER

Total Quality (TQ) is a successful (at least in Japan) management approach that stresses individual responsibility for quality and for the continual improvement that leads to Productive Quality. Many companies in other countries are trying to implement the approach with varying degrees of success. TQ *will* work if implemented properly. The keys of TQ are exactly the same as the three steps and TQ is based on the same operating philosophy. The philosophy is *kaizen* — which translates readily as improvement "a little bit at a time all the time". In TQ, people are selected carefully for their capability to work in a TQ system, they are told explicitly what needs to be done and what their role is, and the system is designed specifically to let them play that role. In short, TQ works well if the three steps are taken — but so do other management approaches.

Many of the basic concepts of TQ are consistent with the way people should perform in any system and it's useful to see how they fit together in a specific operating system. But TQ in its pure form requires a degree of structure and regimentation that many companies will find difficult to digest, and that may be counterproductive in our culture, which gives its highest awards to personal initiative and willingness to try something different. Since any reasonable management approach applied consistently will work if the three steps and the operating framework are used, invest energy in taking those steps rather than implementing complex operating systems.

A MEASURES PRIMER

Part of doing what needs to be done is understanding job measures and learning how to use them to get continual improvement through reduced variation. For meaningful performance measures, people must measure what *they* control. Bottom line results are obtained only if each individual improves *their* performance in *their* role. Individual measures provide the baseline for individual improvement, which leads to bottom line improvement. Everyone should be aware of the priority of bottom line results so decisions to improve those results at the expense of individual results can be made when such trade-offs arise. Measures *are* important, but they are useful only when they *build* on helping individuals achieve specific individual goals that, in turn, help achieve organizational goals. Otherwise they become simply a drill.

HOW TO TAKE THE THREE STEPS

GETTING AND KEEPING
ONLY THE BEST PEOPLE

1. Regularly meet and talk with everyone one-to-one. This tells you who your best and worst performers are, and who wants to do — and can do — what.

2. Always be in a recruiting mode. Good people are too valuable to be pursued only when someone is needed. *Always* be looking — more good people are *always* needed.

3. Recruit people at the highest possible level — at all levels. The person behind the counter is the company to the outside customer. Get the best in every position — it's cost effective to pay enough to get them.

4. Reorganize and rotate regularly on a planned basis. The right person in the right job is the foundation of Productive Quality. Get them there by constantly reorganizing and rotating.

5. Transfer the poorest performers (the lowest 10%) in a permanent flow. This is one of the most important steps; get and *keep* only the best. A key part of keeping the best is transferring the worst — the continual replacement of the lowest 10% keeps the organization's performance level improving continually.

MAKING CLEAR
WHAT NEEDS TO BE DONE

Make clear what is defined as good performance. Encourage people to do the whole job — they are most likely to do so when they operate under the following ground rules:

1. Know who individual customers and suppliers are — the job is to satisfy customers and develop a good working relationship with suppliers (which is necessary to satisfy customers consistently).

2. Develop job measures that lead to continual improvement in what is done for customers.

3. Know how to set achievable goals and achieve them.

4. Be a constructive complainer.

5. Practice the art of communication.

6. Managers should practice management by walking around (MBWA).

Make clear the training that is available and help everyone find the training they need. Not everybody needs every kind of training, but everybody always needs some kind of training. The world changes and people must change with it.

Make clear the results that are expected — tell them more than just the bottom line. How they get the results is important (developing good operating methods is an expected result). Focus on the individual results that drive bottom line results. Ask them consistently about both kinds of results to be sure you get both, and make clear the changes in priorities among different results so people can adjust their individual priorities accordingly. Telling people all results are equally important is worse than not telling them anything at all.

LETTING THEM DO
WHAT NEEDS TO BE DONE

1. Make clear who is responsible for what. Knowing what one is and is *not* responsible for gives the freedom to concentrate — and that's the freedom to succeed. Make clear to service functions that their responsibility is to act as a service and not as a policeforce to operating functions.

2. Attach authority to responsibility — get the decisions made as close to the work as possible. Distribute authority to the places where it can do the most good (the places closest to the work), and avoid micromanaging the use of that authority. Go where the knowledge is — close to the work — when decisions are made about how to orga-

nize the work and how to write procedures to implement company policies. Otherwise the real "hidden plant" is created — the army of system beaters buried in organizations to beat systems that don't work. Get *working* systems by permitting people close to the work to control decisions about how the work is conducted.

3. Analysis that converts data to information is needed. Develop useful information and make it readily available to everyone. Good decisions require good information. Create an atmosphere of trust in which to operate to get data that reflects what is actually happening.

A FINAL WORD

Now that you know what to do and how to do it, act on a very important word — "start." Pick an action that addresses one of your biggest problems and do something now. Today. Then do a little more tomorrow. A little bit at a time. . . .